San Francisco:
The Musical History Tour

Also by the Author

San Francisco:

The Musical History Tour

A Guide to Over 200
of the Bay Area's Most
Memorable Music Sites

by Joel Selvin

Photographs by Keta Bill Selvin,
David F. Selvin, and from the files
of the *San Francisco Chronicle*

CHRONICLE BOOKS
SAN FRANCISCO

Library of Congress
Cataloging-in-Publication
Data:

Selvin, Joel.
San Francisco, the musical
history tour: a guide to
over 200 of the Bay Area's
most memorable music
sites / by Joel Selvin.
    p.   cm.
Includes index.
ISBN: 0-8118-1007-0
1. Popular Music—
California—San Francisco—
History and criticism.
2. Musical landmarks—
California—San Francisco—
Guidebooks.
3. San Francisco (Calif.)—
Guidebooks. I. Title.
ML3477.8.S26S45 1996
781.64'097946—dc20
95-3597   CIP   MN

Printed in the United
States.

Book and cover design:
Mark Jones

Distributed in Canada by
Raincoast Books,
8680 Cambie Street
Vancouver, B.C. V6P 6M9

10 9 8 7 6 5 4 3 2 1

**Chronicle Books
275 Fifth Street
San Francisco, CA 94103**

Chronicle Books® is
registered in the US Patent
and Trademark Office.

To

Ralph J. Gleason and
John L. Wasserman

It's really your beat; I'm just walking it.

Acknowledgments

My thanks, always, go to Art Fein, author of *The LA Musical History Tour*, which can be commended to anyone with an interest in the subject.

At Chronicle Books, my fond appreciation goes to Editor-in-Chief/drummer Nion McEvoy, his associate Charlotte Stone, and Drew Montgomery, who have cheered this project along from the start.

Other researchers who lent time and thoughts include Kevin Walsh, Greil Marcus, Lee Hildebrand, David Plotnikoff, and Nicholas G. Meriwether. Kathleen Rhodes at the *S.F. Chronicle* library was an invaluable associate. Richard Geiger at the *Chronicle* library isn't too bad himself. The San Francisco Public Library, both the San Francisco collection and the periodical reading room, as always, provided the kind of help only great libraries can.

So many people took the time to answer ridiculously miniscule questions that a complete list would be impossible. But a nearly complete list would have to include Bill Frater, Joan Cashell, Ted Gioia, Robert Corona Jr., Dirk Dirksen, Michael Cerchai, Jack Leahy, Richard Olsen, Chet Helms, Cathy Cohn, Brad Gates, Eugene Vrana, Kim Lafleur, David Landis, Karen Cardell, Jimmy Yuell, Jeannie Bradshaw, Ray Ward, Cynthia Bowman, Michelle Saevke, Jean Catino, Peter McQuaid, Dennis McNally, Rico Tee, Dawn Holiday, Brook Spoerry, Toby Gleason, Bill Belmont, Jennifer Whittington, Sandy Klawans, Herb Caen, Robbie Hurwich, Judy Van Austen, Brad Schulenberg, Jim Farley, Bob McClay, Doug Clifford, Jim McCullough, Jeannie Patterson, Pat Thomas, Bob Heyman, Steve Miller, Laura Tibbals, Kirk Hammett, Earl (Speedo) Sims, Dan Dion, Erik Weber, Jeffrey Cohen, Daniel Bacon, John Allair, Mark Bronstein, Tom Diamant, Kevin J. O'Brien, Terry Haggerty, and Bruce Cohn.

CONTENTS

2
Haight-Ashbury

3
Around Downtown

4
The Neighborhoods

5
East Bay

6
North Bay

7
South Bay

Introduction

What started as a salvage operation on surplus research from my history of the
San Francisco rock scene, *Summer of Love,* turned out to have a life of its own. In
addition to the rock music that has flourished in this city since those historic
dance-concerts in fall 1965 at the Longshoremen's Hall, San Francisco has been
home to remarkable musical history since the days of the Barbary Coast.

When young Al Jolson wandered into town, only days after the 1906 earthquake, the town throbbed to a vital rhythm that he incorporated into his musical
life. That Jolson used to sing in a tent on the exact spot where the Grateful Dead
presided over the closing of Winterland some eighty years later speaks to San
Francisco's long, rich romance with the sounds of the day.

The very neighborhood where jazz music took root in this town before
World War I still teems with the sounds of the city. Mere doorways away from
where Al Jolson learned to dance the Texas Tommy, garage rock thrives on the
site of the birth of the Smothers Brothers's comic folk music. Although the exact
structure around the corner that housed the Jupiter Grill, where Jelly Roll
Morton fronted a ten-piece orchestra before the police ran him out of town,
may have vanished into the mists of time, Morton's ghost hovers over the neighborhood, where his descendants—John Coltrane, Miles Davis, and Cannonball
Adderley—left their tracks behind them.

Some jazz historians even point to the florid arrangements of Art Hickman's
dance band at the St. Francis Hotel as the beginning of big band jazz. The so-
called "King of Jazz," bandleader Paul Whiteman, started life as a viola player
in the S.F. Symphony, until another, newer sound, emanating from another
neighborhood, took him over.

It was in San Francisco where Louis Armstrong poked his head into
Jimbo's Bop City to hear—for the first and only time in recorded history—
Charlie Parker play. Satchmo, of course, famously derided the Young Turk sound
of bebop as "Chinese music." And those fabulous beatniks of North Beach in the
fifties, who adopted modern jazz as their national anthem, merrily mixed poetry
and saxophones, folk music and Benzedrine, in a cultural cocktail that changed
the face of a generation. Their traces are somewhat easier to follow than the revelers
who slummed around Barbary Coast saloons after the turn of the century.

To this day, the North Beach neighborhood remains a bristling mélange of different worlds—traditional Chinese, old-fashioned Italian, shadowy bohemians, young punks, sleazy fleshpits. In this long-standing petri dish, young beatniks, drawn from across the country by the lure of Jack Kerouac's *On the Road,* mingled with these streams in the 1960s. Janis Joplin first sang the blues in Grant Avenue coffeehouses where Paul Kantner of the Jefferson Airplane still takes his afternoon espressos.

What always made San Francisco such a rich breeding ground for creativity is exactly this confluence. While nominally about music history, this book includes many sites associated with other cultural feeder streams: the poetry of Allen Ginsberg, the comedy of Lenny Bruce and Steve Martin, the antics of Ken Kesey and his Merry Pranksters. Just as Lenny Bruce took many of his cues from the jazz musicians of his time, rock musicians of the sixties were inspired by Bruce's artful candor and naked self-revelation. These pursuits recognize no boundaries; in San Francisco, they have always flowed together.

The name Haight-Ashbury alone conjures up images of psychedelic drugs and meandering, pulsing rock music. But, again, the cultural revolution fronted by the Jefferson Airplane, Grateful Dead, Quicksilver Messenger Service, Big Brother and the Holding Company and others was not relegated strictly to the musical. Change was in the air, and the lady who flipped Love burgers on Haight Street has a story to tell, which in its own way is as vital and emblematic as any. The old Irish working-class neighborhood has become synonymous around the globe with the sixties in San Francisco, a decade that left an indelible imprint on the area. But San Francisco rock didn't begin or end with the Airplane or the Dead. The tracks of latter-day rockers such as Chris Isaak and Metallica can be found on the same block where the Dead once strung extension cords out of the Straight Theater and played from a flatbed truck.

Southern soul man Otis Redding was charmed enough by the town to inspire his great hit "(Sittin' on the) Dock of the Bay," while staying on a Sausalito houseboat only several hundred yards from where, twenty-five years later, his Memphis musical colleague, organist Booker T. Jones, located his recording studio after moving to the Bay Area. These kinds of threads can be found throughout the story of San Francisco and its music.

This is, by definition, a personal view, an idiosyncratic tour of this city's musical history. No attempt to be comprehensive was even considered. For me it quickly became a way to look at the town's long love affair with music that defied telling in any other way. In the empty spaces where places like the Blackhawk or Jazz Workshop once stood rests a San Francisco that was unique, thrilling, and piquant in a way life never was again. In a room like Bimbo's 365 Club, the past is even stitched into the decor, the architecture, the very atmosphere of the place.

Introduction

The sites in this book have been arranged in rough geographic order to take the reader on a walking tour through the neighborhoods. If someone wanted to actually take the book to the streets and follow the path described, so much the better. But many of the sites described in this guidebook are long gone. Not even the shell of the buildings remain. Still this way of looking at San Francisco's musical past turns out to be a way to pry loose anecdotal chunks of the city's history: to look at the building where the El Cid once stood and see the story of the Beau Brummels and Tom Donahue, to think of Winterland and imagine hearing Pigpen leading the Dead through "In the Midnight Hour" as sisters Joan Baez and Mimi Farina lent their voices to the enterprise. The triumph of Steve Martin, the despair of Lenny Bruce, the passionate cry of Janis Joplin, the last ringing notes of The Beatles playing before an audience, the timid triumph of a young Barbra Streisand and Woody Allen, two unknowns at the hungry i—all these are San Francisco stories.

Giants walked these paths. Their tales should not be lost.

—Joel Selvin
San Francisco, April 1995

1

North Beach

1

2

The Barbary Coast ... beatniks in coffeehouses ...
late-night bebop jam sessions ... Lenny Bruce,
Mort Sahl, and the Smothers Brothers ... Johnny
Mathis ... the topless craze ... Tom Donahue and
the Beau Brummels ... the young Janis Joplin ...
Mike Bloomfield and Friends ... the birth of underground radio ... punk rock San Francisco-style

San Francisco Bay

N

Lombard

Greenwich

Columbus

24, 25, 26

19, 20

21

2

22

23

4, 5, 6, 7

8, 9, 10

13

30

27   Union

31

3

1

16

14

Green

11

Vallejo

12

18

28

15

Broadway

17

29

Pacific

Jackson

Washington

Clay

Mason

Powell

Stockton

Grant

Kearny

Montgomery

34

33

32

North Beach

1 The Condor
2 El Cid
3 Swiss American Hotel
4 El Matador
5 Ann's 440
6 Mother's
7 The Stone
8 Mabuhay Gardens
9 Basin Street West
10 Jazz Workshop
11 Peppermint Tree
12 Vesuvio's
13 Tosca's
14 Purple Onion
15 hungry i

16 Purcell's
    The So Different Club
17 Columbus Recorders
18 North Beach Revival
19 Coffee and Confusion
20 Coffee Gallery
21 Co-Existence Bagel Shop
22 Savoy-Tivoli
23 Stewart Brand Apartment
24 Anxious Asp
25 Gino & Carlo's
26 The Cellar
27 Neal and Carolyn
    Cassady Apartment
28 Orphanage
29 Melvin Belli Offices
30 KMPX Studios
31 Keystone Korner
32 Wolfgang's
33 Bimbo's 365 Club
34 Journey Headquarters

The Musical History Tour

The Condor

300 Columbus Avenue

For twenty years, dancer Carol Doda was synonymous with topless entertainment on Broadway, doing umpteen shows a week on the tiny corner stage of the big nightclub at the intersection of Columbus and Broadway, "where it all started," as The Condor asserted over the years. Doda splashed onto the front pages when press agent Davey Rosenberg, a vulgar, corpulent Runyonesque character, got the idea in 1964 to dress the go-go dancer in one of designer Rudi Gernreich's topless bathing suits, the fashion controversy du jour. San Franciscans followed her silicone injections, her disastrous attempts to crash the big time in New York, and her ultimately desolate exile to a career spent in this one room. But she earned respect for endurance in a field where two years is about the maximum survival rate. All the *paisanos* used to give her the high sign when she dined at the counter of Vanessi's nearby.

Before Doda pulled on that topless swimsuit in 1964, the club was a thriving go-go, home to the famed duo George and Teddy, a pair of black rock and rollers who showed the Righteous Brothers more than a few moves. They cut a couple of experimental albums with record producer Sly Stone for Autumn Records, the North Beach–based record label, but they never amounted to much outside the neighborhood. Bobby Freeman, whose 1958 Top 5 hit, "Do You Want to Dance," distinguished him as San Francisco's first rock star, spent many years spelling Carol Doda with four performances a night at the club. His 1964 hit, "C'mon and Swim," had been the quintessential product of the pre-topless Broadway rock and roll scene—a screaming, deathless groove with lyrics by Sly Stone that he built around a dance invented by go-go dancer Judy Mac down the street at the Galaxy Club in those brief, halcyon days of rock and roll on Broadway.

Doda used to make her exit standing atop a baby grand piano that was hoisted to the ceiling, where she disappeared through a small hole. This legendary instrument made the headlines in 1983 when the club manager and his girlfriend, engaged in after-hours sexplay on the lid, somehow triggered the hydraulic lift and crushed themselves against the roof. The manager died and his cocktail-waitress girlfriend suffered amnesia after lying beneath the dead man for several hours until the janitor happened across the freak accident the next morning.

El Cid

606 Columbus Avenue

A colorful mural of Broadway's past decorates the wall of the building that housed the second best-known topless club on the strip for many years, once home to Gaye Spiegleman, "topless mother of eight," who was later killed in a car crash. Most recently, the building has been the site of a Chinese restaurant. Although the ambience of the club was decidedly seedy in its day, the El Cid managed to attract customers far beyond the usual life of the scene, probably because of the prominent location on the corner across the street from the Condor.

But the club's real claim to fame in rock and roll history lies with disc jockey/entrepreneur Tom Donahue's discovery of the Beau Brummels. "A hooker told me about them," Donahue said, "and I always listen to hookers." Donahue, a colorful, pivotal figure in the history of San Francisco music, was a Top 40 disc jockey fleeing a payola scandal who landed in town in 1961 from Philadelphia. He opened his nightly show on KYA with his trademark dark rumble of a voice with a deathless tagline: "I'm here to clean up your face and mess up your mind."

With partner Bobby Mitchell, Donahue quickly became a kingpin on the local scene, overseeing their burgeoning empire from nearby offices at 54 Martha Street. They produced concerts at the Cow Palace, owned racehorses, ran a nightclub, and lunched daily at an outside table at Enrico's, surrounded by record-company promotion men, where Donahue never, ever picked up the tab. They founded their Autumn Records label initially to sell a 1963 live album made at one of their rock and roll shows, *Memories of the Cow Palace,* featuring performances by the Ronettes, Dee Dee Sharp, the Righteous Brothers, Freddy Cannon, Bobby Freeman, Dionne Warwick, Betty Harris, and George and Teddy in front of an orchestra conducted by the young record producer Phil Spector.

The following year, they crashed the charts with their Bobby Freeman hit "C'mon and Swim," supervised by KDIA deejay Sly Stone, the house producer for Autumn Records, although the Beatles and their successive imitators from England had rendered such basic American rock and roll virtually a dead issue by mid-1964. Enter the Beau Brummels, playing nightly at the El Cid.

Vocalist Sal Valentino grew up in the streets of North Beach (his father used to play stickball with the DiMaggio brothers in the neighborhood). His haunting voice matched guitarist Ron Elliott's songs, and "Laugh, Laugh," the decidedly Brit-styled group's first Autumn Records single, floated into the Top 20 during the first few months of 1965. Donahue always maintained the song would have gone to number one on a label with stronger distribution. The follow-up track, "Just a Little," slid firmly into the Top 10 later the same year, although inventive subsequent singles such as "You Tell Me Why" and "Don't Talk to Strangers" failed to score outside the Bay Area.

Swiss American Hotel
534 Broadway

Whether it was a suicide attempt or a drug-induced accident, Lenny Bruce, stark naked, fell out of the hotel's second-story window into the parking lot below on March 29, 1965. He managed to tumble in midair, landing on his feet, breaking both ankles and smashing his bones into his hips. But he was conscious enough; the hospital attendants taped his mouth shut.

El Matador
492 Broadway

Founded in the early fifties by author/bullfight aficionado Barnaby Conrad, who painted the giant bullfight mural that covered one wall and wrote a book about his days running the club, the El Matador became one of the town's prime jazz showcases fifteen years later under the management of Walter Pastore, a clubier who used to have his sport coats let out to accommodate his shoulder holster. During the Conrad years, 1953 to 1963, the tiny club (capacity: one hundred twenty) was a place for intimate conversation and quiet drinks, overlooked by live parrots. Frank Sinatra, Marlon Brando, Eva Gabor, Paul Newman—all once toddled into the place to have a drink at the bar underneath the head of the bull supposedly killed by Tyrone Power in the movie *Blood and Sand*. Pianist John Horton Cooper often gave up his bench to visiting dignitaries such as Art Tatum, Duke Ellington, Hoagy Carmichael, Erroll Garner, George Shearing, and Noel Coward. Lenny Bruce and Jonathan Winters spent one night in the club trading lines to the great amusement of the small crowd lucky enough to be on hand to witness the historic duel.

When Conrad sold the club in 1963, the musical policy changed from piano to guitar. After the debut of Brasil '65, whose pianist Sergio Mendes later formed the hugely successful Brasil '66, the club featured a string of guitarists: Bola Sete, Jose Feliciano, Charlie Byrd, Wes Montgomery, Barney Kessel, and Juan Serrano. Under Walter Pastore's stewardship, the El Matador hosted the first U.S. nightclub engagement of Michel Legrand. Until Pastore closed the club in 1977, to be able to share the space with the sublime pianistics of Oscar Peterson in the only nightclub the gifted jazzman would play was a transcendant event—even if the bartender kept mixing blender drinks.

Ann's 440

440 Broadway

As unlikely a place as a dingy lesbian hangout may have been for Lenny Bruce to get his big show-business break, Ann's 440 booked the comedian's first major nightclub engagement in January 1958. The club was already known as the hole-in-the-wall where Johnny Mathis was discovered by Columbia Records scout George Awakian in 1953. While on a trip to Los Angeles, owner Ann Dee heard about a potent new comic, Lenny Bruce. He waltzed into San Francisco in the middle of a major cultural upheaval, with the Beats mixing jazz and poetry down the street and Mort Sahl serving notice around the corner at the hungry i that comedy could mean more than one-liners and rim shots. Bruce's routine about a black hipster auditioning for Lawrence Welk may have earned him some wrath from Welk's attorneys, but it also brought him to the attention of Hugh Hefner and Chicago nightclub owners, as he launched his extraordinary career, ironically, across the street from where it would begin to unravel only three years later.

In the eighties, under the hand of the inimitable Miss Keiko and a new name, Chi-Chi Theater, the room played host to some of the Mabuhay Gardens punk-rock spillover in a tinseled setting reminiscent of the little nightclub in the film *Desperately Seeking Susan.*

Mother's

430 Broadway

Folksinger Barbara Dane carved out this room as Sugar Hill, a folk club where she not only recorded a live album of her own but introduced hip San Francisco audiences to blues singers like T-Bone Walker, Mama Yancey, John Lee Hooker, and Lightnin' Hopkins. Under the management of deejays Tom Donahue and Bobby Mitchell in 1965, the club, renamed Mother's, was probably the country's first psychedelic nightclub, with walls covered with flourescent paintings and featuring a light show. They brought in the Lovin' Spoonful just as the band's first single, "Do You Believe in Magic," was breaking big. The club also caught some of the first ballroom bands, like the Grateful Dead, which played an early date at the short-lived club that went out of business within a year, and Great Society, featuring Grace Slick in one of that group's first dates.

The Stone
412 Broadway

Tony Bennett opened this room in 1967 when it was called Mr. D's, an elegant supper club named for Sammy Davis Jr., who had a modest financial interest in the venture. By 1972, the club had passed through several hands before Peter Abrams of the Matrix reopened his historic Fillmore Street club on the premises. The next year club booker Scott Piering took a chance and flew in an unknown group of Jamaican musicians who were stranded in Las Vegas after being fired from a Sly and the Family Stone tour. Called the Wailers, the group surprised everybody—including themselves—by packing the place for two consecutive nights. The band stayed in town to appear again the following weekend, and gave a free radio concert on KSAN that later surfaced on an Island Records CD called *Talkin' Blues*. It was these 1973 club dates at the Matrix that first showed Bob Marley he could be successful in the United States.

The next incarnation of the room was the Soul Train, a joint venture of Oakland-based concert producer Dick Griffey and television personality Don Cornelius, whose "Soul Train" television show was just starting its long and successful run on the airwaves. Their club did not last that long, although, in the short time it did stay open on Broadway, Soul Train played host to a number of great soul shows by the stars of the day like Harold Melvin and the Blue Notes. Comedian Richard Pryor cut a scorchingly funny 1974 live album, *That Nigger's*

From Marley to Metallica, a quarter-century parade of greats crossed the stage at the Stone. (1995, photo by Keta Bill Selvin)

Crazy, during the club's brief tenure. The spoofy play, *Bullshot Crummond*, ran for several years when the room was named the Hippodrome in the late seventies.

But when Freddie Herrera and Bobby Corona took over the lease in 1980 to establish the Stone—Muddy Waters and John Lee Hooker were the opening bill, followed by two nights with the Jerry Garcia Band—the new partnership suddenly represented a small fiefdom of three clubs, including the Keystone-Palo Alto and Keystone Berkeley, able to make serious offers to big-name rock acts for lucrative three-night mini-tours. For the next several years, the Broadway club was a thriving alternative to the Bill Graham–run clubs. (Bobby Corona, in fact, sued Graham for unfair competition and Graham settled out of court.)

The club presented a full array of musical styles. Prince made a memorable 1982 appearance, inciting the entire audience to sing along with his "Head." Muddy Waters, John Lee Hooker, and a young Robert Cray once played a triple bill at the seven hundred-seat club. Soul greats from James Brown and Wilson Pickett to the Four Tops and the Temptations worked the room. Later as a haven for the burgeoning heavy metal/thrash scene, the Stone was one of the few local clubs that would book the young Metallica. Bassist Cliff Burton played his second gig with the band at the club, an event immortalized in the video "Cliff 'Em All."

After ten years, Herrera and Corona split their partnership, having already sold their Palo Alto and Berkeley clubs, and unloaded the lease on John Nady, inventor of the wireless guitar who was already running an Oakland club called the Omni. Nady never enjoyed the success of the Keystone chain, and within a few years he vacated the lease and left a sign on the marquee reading "Bye."

Mabuhay Gardens

443 Broadway

Robin Williams remembered working the Mab. "Tonight is comedy heaven, where everything is funny," Robin Williams exulted during his triumphant headline debut at the Boarding House in 1978, freshly anointed by the success of the television hit "Mork and Mindy." "Comedy hell," he added, "comedy hell is opening for the Ramones at the Mabuhay."

With Eddie Mesa, "the Elvis of the Philippines," serving as the club's long-running attraction, the Mabuhay was doing yeoman's service as a Filipino supper club when television producer Dirk Dirksen walked into the place in 1973 and began presenting shows at the club. Dirksen, a man with an eye for the offbeat, brought the campy shenanigans of Les Nickelettes, a whimsical song-and-dance troupe formed by some employees of the Mitchell Brothers Theater. With Jon Hendricks's jazz musical *Evolution of the Blues* running upstairs at the On Broadway, sound problems caused Dirksen to agree to start his shows at eleven o'clock, after the jazz show ended, making the Mabuhay the scene of the town's early late show. Dirksen collected and showcased fragments of the town's demented edge, such as comics Jane Dornacker and Freaky Ralph.

But his real breakthrough came with the onslaught of punk rock; Dirksen, with his anything goes, let-the-chips-fall attitude, immediately provided a snug harbor in the North Beach nightlife scene for these bands. Canadian iconoclast Mary Monday started the ball rolling, followed shortly by such local scenemakers as the Nuns, the Avengers (featuring guitarist Jimmy Wilsey, later famed for his work with Chris Isaak), and Crime. Dirksen held monthly booking meetings, which included free spaghetti, and let the bands fight among themselves over open dates. With the arrival of East Coast bands like Blondie, the Ramones, Devo, Dead Boys, and others, the Mabuhay reinforced a movement that spanned the nation. Soon, nascent bands like the Go-Go's were packing their gear into creaky vans and making the drive from Los Angeles to play for peanuts and the pure pleasure of belonging to this suddenly thriving scene.

Dirksen played the evil entrepreneur with relish, snarling at the audience between acts: "Quiet down, animals." On his birthday every year, he held a public celebration at the club, in which he staged his own flogging, beheading, and burning at the stake ("Bring a faggot to throw on the fire," read one flyer). He handed out drums of popcorn to encourage popcorn fights, although the scattered kernels left janitors frustrated and attracted mice and cockroaches. One of his great pranks was to answer rumors that the Rolling Stones would play a surprise date at the punk emporium during the band's 1981 tour by booking a group and dubbing the band Tattoo. Hundreds of disappointed fans showed up outside the Mab the night of the gig.

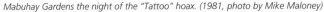

Mabuhay Gardens the night of the "Tattoo" hoax. (1981, photo by Mike Maloney)

North Beach

Basin Street West
401 Broadway

The tiered seating put every patron in the middle of the action at this jazz and soul club, one of the few North Beach jazz joints to admit minors. The room opened in 1964 with the Latin jazz of Eddie Cano and pianist Hampton Hawes and closed in 1973, replaced by a Korean restaurant. Big names from Smokey Robinson and the Miracles to Otis Redding worked the room. Members of Jefferson Airplane sat in with Dizzy Gillespie, and Ike and Tina Turner recorded a live album here. Tired of having police officers do his act on witness stands across the country, Lenny Bruce, defending himself against a plethora of obscenity charges, filmed a documentary of his act at the club in spring 1966. It remains the only visual record of the great comedian's nightclub work.

Jazz Workshop
473 Broadway

Cannonball Adderley put this Broadway club on the jazz map with his October 1959 live session, *In San Francisco*, which yielded the soul hit, "This Here," and prompted a 1962 reprise, *Jazz Workshop Revisited*. The club was home in its earliest days to the Mastersounds, the group featuring the three Montgomery brothers, Monk, Buddy and, occasionally, Wes. After the Blackhawk, the town's top jazz spot, closed in 1963, the Workshop inherited the steady procession of touring acts that included Miles Davis, Art Blakey, Horace

Jazz Workshop: Monk, Miles, Trane, all the rest. (1963, photo by Peter Breinig)

Silver, Sonny Rollins, and their ilk. Saxophonist John Coltrane worked the club all through the sixties, beginning in 1960 following his Monterey Jazz Festival debut with a two-week engagement. His band at the time was a short-lived aggregation that included saxophonist Eric Dolphy and guitarist Wes Montgomery. During this run, local sax man Kermit Scott introduced Coltrane to a young apostle named Farrell Sanders, who would follow the jazz giant's footsteps under the name Pharoah Sanders. In his January 1966 engagement, Coltrane showed up with two drummers and an African percussionist, heralding his experiments with poly-rhythms that were showcased on his famous album, *Meditations.* On October 4, 1961, Lenny Bruce began his show here by describing the clientele at Ann's 440 with a graphic eleven-letter term that led to his first arrest on obscenity charges. Shortly after the 1982 death of Thelonious Monk, Columbia Records unearthed a 1964 live session and issued a double-record set titled *Live at the Jazz Workshop,* more than a decade after the club's closing. Though briefly reprised in recent years, the club got lost amid the massage parlors and topless bars in the area during the late sixties.

Peppermint Tree
660 Broadway

Formerly the location of an after-hours spot called The Celebrity, the Peppermint Tree opened as a rock and roll club with a large dance floor in 1964 with Paul Revere and the Raiders and Jody ("Queen of the House") Miller as the initial attractions. The Byrds played a two-week engagement the next year, bridging the worlds of Top 40 and the new underground rock. Caving in to the topless trend with a novel twist—the Tree featured "amateur" topless dancers—business dipped, so the club brought back name acts in 1967, beginning with Little Richard (whose hotel room was burgled of a cache of his jewelry during the run). Before long, the club concentrated on Top 40 cover bands, with occasional other bookings. Wacky Philly soul singer Bunny Sigler played the club one week in 1973, running out of the club during one number every night and changing costumes on the sidewalk before returning. By 1975, the club stopped booking live bands altogether.

Vesuvio's
255 Columbus Avenue

Francis Ford Coppola reportedly penned major portions of the *Godfather* script while sitting in this quintessentially North Beach joint, one of the few remaining remnants of beatnik North Beach. Owner Henri Lenoir, who previously ran the saloon across the street at 12 Adler Place now known as Specs, opened Vesuvio's in 1949. The place used to sell a "Beatnik Kit" that included a copy of a poem titled, "How Are You Going to Keep Them Down on the Farm After They've Seen North Beach?" Welsh poet Dylan Thomas loved to get drunk at the bar. One fabled night, Jack Kerouac kept phoning author Henry Miller in Carmel from the pay phone to say he would be delayed—they were supposed to meet. Kerouac never left Vesuvio's that night and he and Miller never did meet. Today, the bohemian atmosphere remains. Paul Kantner of Jefferson Airplane can be found at the bar any afternoon, puffing away at his Camels and holding forth with the local cafe society.

Tosca's
242 Columbus Avenue

With decor that remains unchanged since before World War II, this quaint North Beach bar trades on the timeless quality of the opera-laden jukebox, red leather banquettes, and the steamed chocolate milk and brandy beverages the bartenders call cappuccinos. Owner Jeannette Etheredge, whose mother, Madame Bali, catered to the international ballet scene at her famed restaurant, draws the art, film, and music crowd with regularity. At any given time, Francis Ford Coppola can be fixing up pasta in the kitchen, Sam Shepard can be shooting pool in the private back room, or film director Phil Kaufman and his crew might be hanging out after a marathon editing session. Bob Dylan was once thrown out of the usually sedate place, along with a party that included Allen Ginsberg, Lawrence Ferlinghetti, and Peter Orlovsky, although management did not know exactly who they tossed out until they read about it in the newspapers. Whenever the band is in town, U2 makes Tosca's their home away from home.

Purple Onion
140 Columbus Avenue

Made famous by the Kingston Trio, Phyllis Diller, and the Smothers Brothers, the Purple Onion vaulted some of the most famous acts of the fifties to emerge in San Francisco off its small stage. Rod McKuen used to drive to work at the club from Berkeley on a motorcycle, his guitar strapped to his back. Comedian Diller was an Alameda housewife and mother of five when owner Bud Steinhoff hired her for $75 a week in 1954. The Kingston Trio had to audition four times before he gave them a job; they spent the first ten months of their career at the club. Tom and Dick Smothers recorded their first album, *Live at the Purple Onion*, at the club.

Steinhoff, who ran the club from its opening in 1952 until his death in 1989, was in the construction business when he started the club with his brother-in-law. He worked the bar and his wife, Virginia, served the drinks. Originally he planned to call the club the Song Cellar, until he mentioned the idea to neighboring club owner, Enrico Banducci. "That's a terrible name," Banducci told him. "Anything would be better—even the Purple Onion." Steinhoff used to bend down and break an empty bottle with a hammer every time the unknown Jim Nabors would hit a high note. Maya Angelou sang and danced at the club. Vicki Carr and Ketty Lester also worked the room when they were unknowns. By the mid-sixties, however, the club was coasting on its reputation and nightly tour buses deposited a steady stream of tourists on the doorstep. In the early nineties, after Steinhoff's death and the club's sale, the Onion became the North Beach base for a kind of garage-rock renaissance—hosting everything from Mod revivalists to surf instrumentalists.

hungry i
599 Jackson Street

Woody Allen opened for Barbra Streisand in 1963, but the club still lost money on the engagement. The Kingston Trio may have groomed their act across the street at the Purple Onion, but when it came time to record a live album, it was *The Kingston Trio from the hungry i.* Frank Werber, the trio's manager, once worked as a waiter at the club when it was located across the street in the basement of the Columbus Tower, a building he eventually bought. They all worked for Enrico Banducci, the beret-wearing impresario who started the hungry i in 1950 and moved it into its famous location four years later.

Folksinger Stan Wilson was the club's first attraction, but it was comedian Mort Sahl, proving comedy could be more than snappy patter and one-liners, who led a new generation of comics across the stage in front of the brick wall. Shelley Berman, Jonathan Winters, Lenny Bruce, Tom Lehrer, Dick Gregory, Bob Newhart, May and Nichols, and Bill Cosby all followed Sahl into the cellar. (Professor Irwin Corey and Banducci once chased a thief who robbed the door-man of five hundred dollars three blocks down the street together before giving up the chase.) By 1968, Sahl's obsession with finding a conspiracy behind the Kennedy assassination made Sahl a show-business pariah. "Banducci is practically the only guy in America who will hire me now," he said. But even Banducci had his limits. One night, in frustration, he simply turned off the spotlight and told Sahl to go home. They didn't speak for more than thirteen years.

In addition to the Kingston Trio, music groups including the Limelighters, the Gateway Singers, Josh White, Miriam Makeba, and the Smothers Brothers all passed through the celebrated showroom. Even Banducci's staff added to the

*hungry i owner
Enrico Banducci with
comic Mort Sahl
before the split.
(1958, photo by
Bill Young)*

31

joint's basement bohemian luster: tall, gaunt Harry Smith, the maitre d'; black-listed Hollywood screenwriter Alvah Bessie, the announcer; and children's television show host David Allen, the club manager.

The hungry i never made the transition to rock, although the Lovin' Spoonful played the club in 1966 during the same week the band headlined the second Family Dog dance-concert at Longshoremen's Hall. The new music sweeping the scene in the sixties turned the club into an anomaly before its time. In the end, Banducci, already operating the Broadway cafe bearing his first name, closed down the old club in 1968 and opened an expensive new dinner-theater on Ghirardelli Square that didn't last long. Eventually, he sold the name, hungry i, to a topless club, lost the restaurant, and left town without a dime to show for it.

Purcell's The So Different Club
520 Pacific Street

Although the building shell still stands, the facade and address have changed. But this was the site of the Barbary Coast's most famous black dance hall. Opened in one of the first buildings erected after the 1906 fire by Lew Purcell and Sam King, a pair of ex-Pullman porters, Purcell's was the hot spot of the Pacific Street strip, a swinging, wide-open nightlife belt bristling with musicians drawn from New Orleans to play new jazz music. It was here that Al Jolson first learned the dance Texas Tommy. King Oliver and his Creole Jazz Band played in 1921, following a brief engagement at the Pagola on Market Street. Ferde Grofé, composer of "Grand Canyon Suite," worked down the street as second pianist at the Hippodrome and always maintained that "the new music of Pacific Street" left a lasting impression on him.

Columbus Recorders

906 Kearny Street

In the basement of the copper cupola now owned by Francis Ford Coppola, where old-time San Francisco political boss Abe Ruef once had his offices, the Grateful Dead pieced together the wild montage that would be the band's second album, *Anthem of the Sun.* Spliced together from dozens of live recordings, previous studio sessions, and some overdubbing done here, the album ran without break over each of its two sides, seamlessly blending song into song in an attempt to capture the extemporaneous nature of the band's live performances. Engineer Richard Beggs has continued to keep the studio in operation, although now he mostly does work on Coppola's movies.

Coffee and Confusion: Janis Joplin did her Bessie Smith number here. (1969, photo by Peter Breinig)

North Beach Revival
1024 Kearny Street

As the Off Broadway, the club once hummed to the sounds of Stan Kenton and Trini Lopez. Lenny Bruce worked the room, but that was before topless took over in the sixties. In 1971, funded by the flush folks at North Beach Leather, the club was reopened as North Beach Revival and tried to introduce the latest rock bands. Dr. Hook and the Medicine Show used to play the club until the band's first album was released. In the eighties, under the name Morty's, the club served as a self-conscious showcase for local alternative rock groups who banded together in a loose affiliation known as ACME. The Himalayans were part of this group, out of which sprang vocalist Adam Duritz, later with the Counting Crows.

Coffee and Confusion
1339 Grant Avenue

Another folk and espresso joint where Janis Joplin used to do her Bessie Smith thing in 1963, Coffee and Confusion lasted into the early seventies, by which time it was an anachronistic remnant of the street's beatnik past.

Coffee Gallery
1353 Grant Avenue

As the Lost and Found Saloon, this slightly seedy club continues a fine neighborhood tradition established in the early sixties when the Coffee Gallery was a fixture on the upper Grant folk scene. Bop saxophonist Pony Poindexter ran the house combo in the late fifties, and the joint hosted a benefit one night in 1960 to raise money for a sprinkler system in a nearby club, The Cellar. The six-hour jam session featured everything from Jimmy Rushing belting the blues to Duke Ellington reciting poetry. Cousin Jimbo from Jimbo's Bop City served as doorman for the occasion, and Enrico Banducci of the hungry i poured drinks.

Although occasional talent from out-of-town passed through the club—comedians Lord Buckley and Hugh Romney (later better known by his *nom de hippie*, Wavy Gravy) played here—it was the North Beach music hopefuls who commanded the stage most of the time. Rock was rarely featured, although the Great Society, the early S.F. rock group featuring Grace Slick, made its first public appearance at the club. Long before her days with a rock band, Janis Joplin sang country blues, one of thousands of young unknown folkies to play at the Coffee Gallery over the years. Many years later, by which time the club had changed hands and its name to the Lost and Found, Led Zeppelin's Robert Plant and band wandered in on an off night from touring and soon took over the bandstand from the everyday blues band that was booked for the evening, delivering a rocking blues jam, much to the astonishment of the dozen or so customers watching.

Co-Existence Bagel Shop
1398 Grant Avenue

Central headquarters of the Beats on Grant Avenue, the Bagel Shop—whose only connection to actual bagels was the one that hung around the overhead lamp cord as a decoration—closed in 1960, signaling the end of an era. This gathering place of the lost generation drew the antipathy of the police, who targeted the beer bar for raids in a long campaign to get the establishment's license revoked. The bulletin board served as the nerve center of the small community. The jukebox featured exclusively progressive jazz, and the place was open for coffee and sandwiches until four in the morning on weekends.

Savoy-Tivoli
1434 Grant Avenue

Before the anti-noise ordinance beat him into the ground, Stephen Gordon ran an intriguing little nightclub for a little more than a year through 1976 in the back room of this Grant Street institution, where the long-running musical *Beach Blanket Babylon* started out. Gordon leased the windowless back room for $90 a month and quickly carved a small but respectable niche for himself on the town's active nightclub scene. One memorable week, he presented a four-night run by Southside Johnny and the Asbury Jukes, the great bar band's S.F. debut, followed by a one-nighter by another new figure in the city, Graham Parker. British soul man Robert Palmer, punk rockers the Ramones, and singer-songwriter Michael Franks all made their local debuts in the tiny room that year. Blues great Jimmy Reed died quietly in owner Gordon's bed after playing the club. When Muddy Waters appeared later, all Gordon wanted was for him to survive the engagement.

Stewart Brand Apartment
9 Margrave Place

Stewart Brand, who later created the *Whole Earth Catalog*, was producer of the Trips Festival, a Merry Pranksters bacchanal, set to take place the weekend of January 21–22, 1966. Three nights before, Ken Kesey and his girlfriend, Mountain Girl, visited Brand, and went up on his rooftop. Kesey had been sentenced to six months in jail for a marijuana possession charge in San Mateo County only two days earlier. As he and Mountain Girl tossed pebbles at the toilet their friend and Brand's neighbor Margot St. James used as a planter outside her adjacent window, they happened to look down into the alley and marveled at the blinking red light on top of the police car parked in front of the apartment building. But nothing could have been more surprising to the pair when the cops burst upon them and found a small bag of pot. Kesey and one of the police struggled over the pouch and Kesey managed to throw the bag off the roof, adding resisting arrest to his charges. The bag and its contents were retrieved and Kesey, now facing serious prison time on pot charges, became a fugitive from justice shortly after attending that weekend's festivities at Longshoremen's Hall.

Anxious Asp
528 Green Street

Janis Joplin used to while away the afternoons drinking and playing pool during the late sixties at this Beat-generation hangout, where Jack Kerouac once read his poetry and the bathroom walls were papered with pages of the Kinsey Report.

Gino & Carlo's
548 Green Street

Locals most frequently recall this old-fashioned sports bar with portraits of fifties boxers adorning the walls as the place where the late *Chronicle* columnist Charles McCabe composed his daily newspaper piece at the corner of the bar, but Janis Joplin also loved to shoot pool in the back room of this neighborhood institution.

The Cellar

576 Green Street

In February 1957, poets Kenneth Rexroth and Lawrence Ferlinghetti tried
reciting their poems against the backdrop of a live jazz quartet downstairs at The
Cellar, unintentionally creating the crucial archetype of the beatnik era. It earned
the tiny club, which opened in 1956 on the former premises of a Chinese restaurant, notices in *Time, Life,* and *Down Beat* magazines. Fantasy Records recorded
an album of Ferlinghetti and Rexroth reading to a jazz trio, *Poetry Readings at the
Cellar.* Jack Kerouac used The Cellar for a scene in his book *Desolation Angels.*
In fact, the place played an incidental role in inciting Rexroth's lifelong antipathy
for Kerouac. Kerouac and poet Robert Creeley were thrown out of the club one
night in 1956 after returning from dockside, where they had bid adieu to poet
Gary Snyder who was on his way to Japan. Kerouac asked Creeley if he would
like to spend the night at Snyder's Mill Valley cabin and Creeley agreed, who
bringing with him Rexroth's wife, Marthe Rexroth. Rexroth himself always
thought it was Kerouac who extended the invitation to Marthe.

*Beats in the base-
ment at the Cellar.
(1958, photo by
Gordon Peters)*

Neal and Carolyn Cassady Apartment
29 Russell Street

In this small alleyway off Hyde Street between Union and Green streets, Jack Kerouac lived in the attic of the home of Neal and Carolyn Cassady, a relationship later commemorated in a highly romanticized feature film, *Heart Beat.* During the winter of 1951–52, Kerouac and Cassady worked on the Southern Pacific Railroad and Kerouac wrote portions of *Visions of Cody, Doctor Sax,* and *On the Road.* It was a blissful time for the author. "It rained every day," he later wrote, "and I had wine, marijuana, and once in a while, Neal's wife would sneak in."

Orphanage
870 Montgomery Street

Under the name the Roaring Twenties, the club was known during the topless days for "The Girl on the Swing," where comely young ladies would swing over the stairwell in the center of the room. The Charlatans played a memorable engagement for several weeks during 1966, when the club briefly experimented with a rock format. Drummer Dan Hicks remembers getting hit in the head with an ashtray thrown at the band by a disgruntled customer, who was more accustomed to gawking at female pulchritude than watching a stylized old-timey rock band.

As the Orphange, however, the club became North Beach's premier rock spot for a hot minute during the early seventies, a kind of cocaine speakeasy that fostered the early career of Graham Central Station, the funky soul band led by Sly and the Family Stone bassist Larry Graham Jr. The band had crowds waiting on the sidewalk to get in before it even released its first album. Mick Jagger and Keith Richards showed up during the wee hours to catch reggae greats Toots and the Maytals one night in 1975, the same year that friends of deejay Tom Donahue gathered at the club to hold a wake. The Tubes played without costumes or makeup for the first time that night and Peter Yarrow (of Peter, Paul and Mary), of all people, opened the event, which lasted until the early morning hours of the next day.

Melvin Belli Offices
722-728 Montgomery Street

In a scene captured in the film *Gimme Shelter,* the famed lawyer, representing the Rolling Stones as the band's plans to hold a free concert to culminate a 1969 U.S. tour began to unravel, received a phone call in his office from one Dick Carter. The manager of an obscure, financially beleagured racetrack called Altamont Speedway, Carter was looking for some publicity and offered the Stones his track for their concert.

KMPX Studios
50 Green Street

The birthplace of underground radio, the second-floor studio of KMPX was always open to visitors and a small crowd often hung out in the lobby while the disc jockeys did their thing behind a glass panel. Larry Miller started broadcasting Bob Dylan, Ravi Shankar, and other records not being played on AM radio on the all-night time slot on this otherwise foreign-language station in February 1967. In April, ex-KYA kingpin Tom Donahue took over the evening shift before Miller's and by the end of the summer the station was full-time underground rock and making waves in the ratings. In March 1968, the entire staff walked out on strike, protesting the absence of pay increases while the station's revenue had exploded eightfold. After announcing the impending walkout over the air for hours prior, the staffers strolled out at midnight to be greeted like champions by a huge crowd waiting outside. Before long, the Grateful Dead rolled up on a flatbed truck and, with Steve Winwood and Jim Capaldi of Traffic on hand, jammed away into the early morning hours. Before two months had elapsed, the strikers were all back at work—at another radio station, KSAN.

Keystone Korner
750 Vallejo Street

Owner Freddie Herrera was sleeping in his station wagon parked in the alley in back and his wife worked as the club's only topless dancer when a rather inebriated Nick Gravenites, songwriter, raconteur, and bon vivant, wandered into the off-the-beaten-path, dingy Keystone Korner in 1969. "What you need is some music," he told Herrera. "I'll bring my friends down next weekend." With his topless bar operating four blocks away from the action on Broadway, Herrera wasn't having any more luck attracting patrons than the previous owners, who named the place Dino Carlo's, had when they tried their hand at booking rock music with some unknown East Bay band called Creedence Clearwater Revival and failed. Herrera, who didn't know Gravenites from Adam, agreed and had no idea that his "friends" would turn out to be superstar guitarist Mike Bloomfield and most of the recently disbanded Electric Flag, who packed the joint to the walls and beyond every weekend under the name Mike Bloomfield and Friends.

Another one of Gravenites's friends, Elvin Bishop, recently departed from The Paul Butterfield Blues Band, was putting together his own group and looking for a place to play. Herrera gave him Monday nights and served free fried chicken to the crowd. The place was packed every Monday and Bishop delighted in hosting freewheeling jam sessions. A sixteen-year-old guitar whiz from the Peninsula made his way up onstage one Monday night, and that's how Neal Schon first splashed down on the S.F. music scene (he later joined Santana and helped form Journey). The Pointer Sisters, preacher's kids from Oakland, started out singing background vocals with Bishop on Monday nights.

The San Francisco music scene supplied so much music talent at the time that even a relative amateur like Herrera couldn't fail. When Bloomfield and Gravenites brought Chicago blues guitarslinger Otis Rush to San Francisco to produce an album, they ran him through Keystone for several nights. Groups sprouted up, such as the New Riders of the Purple Sage, a country-and-western Grateful Dead sideline band, and Boz Scaggs, a former rhythm guitarist with the Steve Miller Band, and into Keystone they headed. The small room accommodated as many as two hundred people, so even off nights drew decent crowds. Within two years, Herrera took over a much larger room in Berkeley and, even though a loose-knit group featuring organist Merl Saunders, Dead guitarist Jerry Garcia, and ex-Creedence guitarist Tom Fogerty still filled the North Beach room every weekend, Herrera sold the small club for a modest $12,500 ($5,000 down) in July 1972 to Todd Barkan, who immediately changed the booking policy to jazz. Soon Barkan was bringing in big-name jazz players like Sonny Rollins and Art Blakey who hadn't played that neck of the woods since the Jazz Workshop closed its doors several years before.

Barkan established Keystone Korner as one of the country's top jazz nightspots. Rahsaan Roland Kirk cut one of his finest albums, a double-record set titled *Bright Moments,* at the club. Keystone developed a nationwide reputation as one of the last great jazz clubs on the West Coast and, as a consequence, Barkan was able to convince many big-name players to work the two hundred-seat club, including McCoy Tyner, Stan Getz, Pat Metheny, Bill Evans, and Miles Davis.

But the financial burden of supporting a full-time jazz club soon overwhelmed Barkan, who was only able to buy a liquor license with funds raised from a 1975 Paramount Theater jam session featuring Kirk, Tyner, Freddie Hubbard, Elvin Jones, and Ron Carter. By 1983, Barkan had virtually run aground. He owed $50,000 in back taxes and arranged another benefit for the club, featuring Manhattan Transfer, Richie Cole, Jon Hendricks, and Bobby McFerrin at the Warfield Theater. When the Bill Graham–produced benefit earned a paltry $1,500 after expenses, Barkan threw in the towel and moved to New York, a bitter, disappointed man.

Wolfgang's
901 Columbus Avenue

Chuck Johnston, one of the kids in the original *Our Gang* comedies, bought into the foundering Italian Village on the site in 1953 after a fire had ravaged the premises. He rebuilt and reopened the Village in August 1956 with Johnnie Ray as his attraction. He didn't have much luck. Abbott and Costello were booked for three weeks, but were bought off after a week. He tried old-timer Sophie Tucker and stripper Lili St. Cyr, but he was gone before a year was up. The club changed hands many times, trying out different recipes, none working. The room hosted weekly twist parties during the dance's craze in the sixties. During the disco era fifteen years later, it went by the name Dance Yer Ass Off.

David Allen then leased the premises and renamed it the Boarding House but went belly-up in 1982 at the rather sumptuous venue he had spruced up considerably only two years before. Chased out of the 960 Bush Street place he had inhabited for eight years by the wrecker's ball, Allen had precious little luck at his beautiful new club. He booked a few good comedy shows—his loyal standby, Lily Tomlin, did a couple of weeks' worth of capacity crowds—but, finally, his only remaining option after a decade of dodging bills and charming creditors was insolvency.

After Allen and the Boarding House vacated the premises, owner Jeffrey Pollack, who made a small bundle selling his Old Waldorf to Bill Graham, operated the place as Bal Tabarin and eventually managed to interest Graham in buying a second nightclub from him. On July 4, 1983, after closing the Old Waldorf, Graham reopened the Columbus Avenue room, doing nothing more than slapping on a fresh coat of paint, buying a new $30,000 sound system, and giving the club his own real first name, Wolfgang's.

Almost immediately, the six-hundred-seat club with the sweeping balcony established itself as the city's top room. In the first year alone, the club boasted acts as varied as songwriter John Hiatt, Aussie new wavers Midnight Oil, U2 impressionists Big Country, professional naif Pee Wee Herman, guitarist Ry Cooder, Angela Bowie (David Bowie's ex-wife), and South African rockers Juluka.

Spinal Tap made a memorable appearance at the club; management handed out "All Excess" backstage passes. Randy Newman and Todd Rundgren gave delightful solo shows. Unknowns Michael Bolton and Sandra Bernhardt drew slim crowds to their local debuts at the club. Bobcat Goldthwaite performed regularly, long before he was known outside San Francisco. Tower of Power and David Lindley were frequent attractions at the club. Nick Lowe appeared one night, while Huey Lewis amused himself at the bar, quietly playing along on harmonica.

Like Pollack, who had run one of the town's first new-wave discos, known as X's, on the site, Wolfgang's management instituted "Dance Dance Dance" programs on Saturdays, when deejays spun records and as many as a thousand dancers a night passed through the doors. Sam Moore of Sam and Dave was the subject of a television-show taping at the club in 1987, where performers as diverse as Dave Edmunds, Roy Orbison, Carla Thomas, Donovan, Mick Fleetwood, Billy Preston, and Jeffrey Osborne all joined Moore onstage. Although the deal to complete the proposed TV program eventually fell through, the evening ranked among the great nights at the club.

On July 31, 1987, a fire broke out in the pensioner's hotel above the club. The four-alarm blaze burned most of the club's ceiling, wiring, and electrical equipment, and the water pumped from fire hoses into the upstairs level finished the job. Wolfgang's closed forever.

Bimbo's 365 Club
1025 Columbus Avenue

An authentic relic of nightlife's golden era, Bimbo's 365 Club freezes time at the moment of the club's 1952 opening. The red-and-black checkerboard carpeting, the parquet dance floor, the leather booths and red tablecloths that decorate the main showroom belong to a bygone time, when Agostino (Bimbo) Giuntoli presided over an array of showgirls, dancers, and crooners that history has since forgotten.

From 1931 to 1951, he operated the town's liveliest speakeasy and after-hours gambling club at 365 Market Street before taking over the former site of Bal Tabarin and polishing the building into a precious gem of a nightclub. Bimbo himself retired in 1970 and, save for private party rentals, closed the club. But in 1988 his grandson, Michael Cerchiai, brought back live entertainment to the glamorous Art Deco confines and made the club home to the famous girl in the fishbowl, restoring San Francisco nightlife's most glittering jewel.

In the beginning a young unknown Rita Hayworth danced in the Bimbo's chorus line. Accordion king Dick Contino announced his wedding engagement during his run at the club. Maestro Arthur Fiedler of the Boston Pops was photographed trying out the latest dance craze at Bimbo's Twist Room. Xavier Cugat with Charo, Louis Prima, Sid Caesar, Ray Anthony, Joey Bishop, Al Martino,

Rusty Draper, Esquivel, Nelson Eddy, Rodney Dangerfield, Totie Fields—they all played the club in its heyday. Latter-day pop sensations like Smokey Robinson and the Miracles, Marvin Gaye, Neil Diamond, Glen Campbell, and The Fifth Dimension were also Bimbo's attractions during the late sixties.

During the years the room was available only as a rental for outside promoters, David Allen of the Boarding House took over the premises for a remarkable run in 1975 by The Tubes, who gave standing-room-only shows that Allen kept extending week after week when the band was the hottest thing on the San Francisco rock scene. Iggy Pop played a memorable show wearing boots and bikini briefs to a slim crowd. When he dived into the small clot of fans in front of the stage, someone dispensed with the briefs and proceeded to minister to Iggy's member. Pop yelled profanities at the woman as he climbed back onstage.

"Holiday in Rio," a typical splashy Bimbo's floor show. (1960, photo by Ralph D. Demeree)

North Beach

An annual fundraiser beginning in 1992 for an Oakland teen drug-treatment program called Thunder Road has presented such performers as Bonnie Raitt, Van Morrison, Steve Miller, Robert Cray, Chris Isaak, Huey Lewis, and others in the intimate confines of the seven hundred-seat club for informal performances. Owner Cerchiai has also brought a South of Market sensibility to the reopened club's booking policy, mixing alternative rock and rhythm and blues with retro-chic that draws a young, dressed-up crowd pretending it is the forties all over again. The era of bare-breasted showgirls wearing bird cages on their heads has long passed and revues like "Holiday in Rio" or "French Follies" are only faint memories. Bimbo's, however, remains.

Journey Headquarters
1111 Columbus Avenue

When *Escape* made Journey one of the most popular rock bands on the planet in 1981, the group's management began looking for a building that would house the entire, Leviathan operation that had grown up around the band, fulfilling everything from graphic-arts design to long-distance trucking for the multi-platinum rock band. This one-of-a-kind building, located by itself on a little triangular island between Columbus and Taylor Streets, was built as a showplace by the trade association for the redwood industry. Every floor contained a different kind of redwood paneling and the conference room had an enormous table made of one giant slab of redwood. Herbie Herbert, the band's manager, oversaw this vast empire from his penthouse suite with its rooftop gardens, where he and cronies frequently repaired for herbal meditation. When the band's fortunes sagged, the business structure was pared down to a more realistic size and Journey sold the building—at a comfortable profit—to the Indonesian consulate.

2

2 Haight-Ashbury

The hippies ... free concerts in the Park ...
Jefferson Airplane ... Grateful Dead ...
Big Brother and the Holding Company ...
the Charlatans ... Family Dog ... psychedelic
posters and underground newspapers ...
Jimi Hendrix ... the Human Be-In ...
Neil Young and Pearl Jam

1 Polo Fields Concert
2 Jerry Garcia
▼ Grace Slick

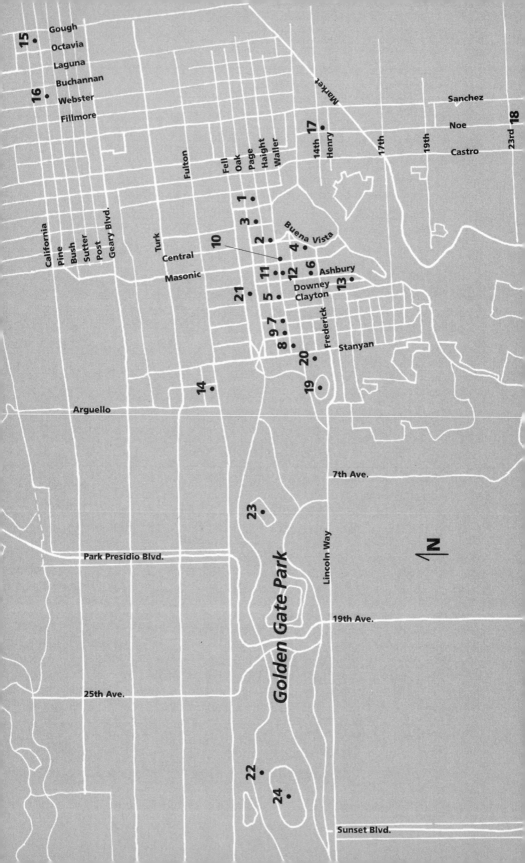

Gough
Octavia
Laguna
Buchannan
Webster
Fillmore

15
16

Sanchez
Noe
Castro
18
23rd
19th
17th

Market
14th
Henry
17

Fulton
Fell
Oak
Page
Haight
Waller

1
3
2
Buena Vista
4
6
Ashbury
10
11
12
Downey
13

California
Pine
Bush
Sutter
Post
Geary Blvd.
Turk
Central
Masonic

21
5
Clayton

9 7
8
20
Frederick
Stanyan
19

14

Arguello

7th Ave.

23

Park Presidio Blvd.

Lincoln Way

19th Ave.

Golden Gate Park

25th Ave.

22
24

Sunset Blvd.

N

Haight-Ashbury

The Musical History Tour

Albin Rooming House
1090 Page Street

Rodney Albin talked his uncle into letting him run the huge Victorian, sprouting bay windows and peaked gables, as a rooming house in 1964. His uncle and some partners had bought the giant house on the corner as an investment, and nobody minded young Albin bringing in a little extra money to help with the payments. Built in 1898, the six-bedroom house had been converted somewhere along the way to accommodate twenty-five Irish-American workers. Albin and his brother, Peter, both bluegrass musicians who attended S.F. State, soon filled the place with students.

In the basement was a rosewood-paneled ballroom, complete with proscenium stage, where Chet Helms, a regular on the weekend party circuit, began to throw Wednesday night jam sessions, charging fifty cents for admission. The house band that grew out of these free-for-alls eventually took the name Big Brother and the Holding Company, although the original members of Quicksilver Messenger Service also jammed at 1090 Page. Sopwith Camel also got its start here. Big Brother moved on, but Rodney Albin continued to operate the rooming house for several years, quitting long before the house fell prey to the wrecker's ball to make way for the condominiums that stand on its former site.

Funky Features
142 Central Avenue

Jack (Funky Jack) Leahy intended to build a private recording studio in the basement of this Victorian, but he spent so much money that he had to open it for business in 1969. With members of Big Brother and the Holding Company living across the street, he quickly attracted a clientele. Producer David Rubinson began bringing some of his Fillmore Records acts such as Cold Blood into the studio. When the Hoodoo Rhythm Devils, a band Leahy managed, landed a contract with Capitol Records, they spent their advance loading a sixteen-track board into the studio. Steve Miller cut his vocals for "Fly Like an Eagle" here. In 1976, a handyman whom Leahy let sleep in the basement stabbed his secretary to death and attacked Leahy and his wife with an axe while they lay sleeping in bed. Leahy had just released his latest album with the Hoodoos, the cover picture taken in his living room upstairs, ironically titled *Safe in Their Homes*. In 1979, Leahy moved his operation uptown to his new Russian Hill Recording; the Haight-Ashbury Victorian was taken over by the Jimi Hendrix Electric Church, an eccentric museum run by a rabid fan and briefly open to the public in the seventies.

Janis Joplin Apartment
112 Lyon Street, No. 3

When Big Brother and the Holding Company moved back to San Francisco from Lagunitas in early 1967, manager Julius Karpen found this apartment for the band's vocalist, a small one-bedroom with a sunny, curving balcony off the front room. Joplin shared the apartment with Country Joe McDonald during their brief affair that spring and was living here when the band made its breakthrough appearance at the Monterey Pop Festival. She was evicted more than a year later because the landlord discovered she owned a dog, George, after spending most of the winter of 1968 in New York recording the band's first album, *Cheap Thrills.*

Janis Joplin's apartment where she lived with Country Joe. (1995, photo by Keta Bill Selvin)

Graham Nash Home

737 Buena Vista West

Through the seventies heyday of Crosby, Stills and Nash, vocalist Graham Nash quietly resided in this Victorian mansion, built in 1897 for Richard Spreckels, nephew of the sugar magnate. Previous residents included journalist Ambrose Bierce and writer Jack London, who wrote his classic *White Fang* in the rambling house. In the sixties, the landmark Victorian housed a small recording studio, run by Gene Estabrook, where many local bands made experimental recordings. Quicksilver Messenger Service and the Steve Miller Band both made their earliest-released records for the soundtrack to the film *Revolution* at the eight-track studio. After Nash sold the house, it was operated for a while as a bed-and-breakfast before actor Danny Glover purchased it as a private residence.

Graham Nash Home. (1995, photo by Keta Bill Selvin)

Haight-Ashbury Free Medical Clinic

558 Clayton Street

A fixture on the street since the sixties, not to mention a presence at every Bill Graham Presents rock concert, the Free Clinic treated members of Nirvana for the flu during their visit to the city in 1989. Band members noticed the clinic's citywide campaign urging drug users to "bleach your works," and decided to name the album the band had recently finished recording *Bleach*.

Grateful Dead House

710 Ashbury Street

The unofficial City Hall of Haight-Ashbury, the Dead House served not only as home to band members Jerry Garcia, Bob Weir, Pigpen, and managers Rock Scully and Danny Rifkin, along with assorted other associates, but contained the office of H.A.L.O. (Haight-Ashbury Legal Organization) as well. Rifkin was the first to move into the house. He managed the building while living in the basement apartment of the three-story Victorian and attending S.F. State. One by one, during the fall of 1966, after the group returned from a brief exodus to Los Angeles and spent the summer in the wilds of Marin's Rancho Olompali, he moved members of the band into empty rooms as they became available, starting with Pigpen to encourage vacancies. The huge house became a kind of community center. In October 1967, police swooped down on the dwelling in a drug raid that netted only a small amount of marijuana. Cops arrested everybody on the premises (Garcia and his girlfriend eluded capture because they were out shopping at the time) including band members Weir and Pigpen, the only non–pot smoking members of the Dead. In March 1968, as a kind of farewell gesture to the neighborhood before the band retreated to Marin, the group sauntered down the hill and played a gig from a flatbed truck stretched across Haight Street, power lines running out of the Straight Theater supplying the electricity.

Guitarist Bob Weir under arrest at the Grateful Dead House. (1967, photographer unknown)

The Musical History Tour

Straight Theater
1702 Haight Street

Converting the old neighborhood movie palace originally built in 1910 took more than a year. But for a brief spell beginning in fall 1967, the Straight provided the Haight with its own dance hall, a hippie-owned and -operated venture, a community-minded alternative to the Fillmore and Avalon that was as hapless as it was well-intentioned. Three hippie partners raised the money for renovation from a variety of investors, including drug dealers, reprobates, miscreants, even Jay Ward, producer of TV's "The Rocky and Bullwinkle Show." One of the partners was the stepson of actress Dame Judith Anderson, who lent her eminence on behalf of the enterprise at one point, testifying before a city permit board. Volunteer labor, worth every penny, did much of the work. Speed freaks behind power sanders smoothed the dance floor until there were ripples in the surface. Acid king and sound engineer Augustus Owsley Stanley installed a state-of-the-art public address system. The Dead used the place as a neighborhood rehearsal hall long before it opened and played during the opening weekend in July 1967. Also appearing that first weekend were Quicksilver Messenger Service, Big Brother and the Holding Company, Country Joe and the Fish, and The Charlatans. For a period, the Straight lost its dance permit, so they offered dance lessons with the Dead as one of the "instructors." Drummer Mickey Hart sat in with the band during a show in September 1967 and never left. One of the up-and-coming bands of the era most associated with the theater was the Santana Blues Band, whose rough-and-tumble mix of blues, rock, and salsa got its real start at the place. The venture ran out of steam in less than a year-and-a-half and closed. Ten years later, the boarded-up derelict theater fell victim to the wrecker's ball.

Nightbreak
1821 Haight Street

Chris Isaak returned to this tiny club on many occasions to hammer out material he planned to record. Prior to both his second and third albums, he booked several nights at the club, strung his plastic tiki lights across the stage, and tried out pieces he was taking into the studio in coming weeks. He also played several nights here following the release of his 1985 debut album, in what was a sentimental return to a place he no longer needed to play. The club also played a large role in the forming of 4 Non Blondes and offered an impromptu stage for jam sessions featuring members of groups like Primus, Metallica, and Faith No More.

I-Beam

1748 Haight Street

Housed in the old Masonic Temple, the I-Beam originally started life at the height of "Saturday Night Fever" as a popular gay disco, run by former astronomer Dr. Sanford Kellman. The spot also ran a series of Sunday afternoon tea dances. But beginning with Monday night shows in 1980 promoted by deejay Alan Robinson, the upstairs room surrounded by pillars grew to be the city's top outlet for imported modern rock through the eighties. The list of new-wave bands that worked the room reads like a Who's Who of the genre—Duran Duran, New Order, Siouxsie and the Banshees, The Cure, R.E.M., The Ramones, Gang of Four, The Buzzcocks, Hüsker Dü, The Replacements, Red Hot Chili Peppers, Terence Trent D'Arby, Living Colour, Jane's Addiction, and 10,000 Maniacs. Faith No More inaugurated the weekend live-music series. Dr. Kellman, dispirited over the death from AIDS of his longtime lover, sold the place in 1990 and the club staggered on for another couple of years. Counting Crows made a notable 1991 appearance at the club in one of the band's first live performances, attended by a number of record-company executives in town for a radio convention. The bidding war for the band started the next morning.

The I-Beam entrance on Haight Street. (1992, photo by Eric Luse)

The Oracle
1371 Haight Street

As much a philosophic treatise as a news broadsheet, the rainbow-colored underground tabloid, *San Francisco Oracle*, was published out of these offices sporadically from 1966 to 1968. Editors Allen Cohen and Michael Bowen were accorded a status of community leaders in the new hippie uprising and helped produce the great Human Be-In on January 1967 at the Polo Fields. More than just another underground rag, the *Oracle* was such a treasured relic that a hardbound twenty-fifth anniversary collection of facsimiles was published and is still available at bookstores along Haight.

Pall Mall Lounge
1568 Haight Street

"For me, the Haight died the day I saw this sleazy, greasy little restaurant advertising 'Love Burgers,'" said Bill Graham. As was often the case, Graham didn't know half the story. The short-order grill concession in the old Pall Mall bar was leased to a flamboyant redheaded Iranian woman who knew nothing of the neighborhood when she arrived. She quickly fell in with the new community and her new customers renamed her Love. She picked up the beat, calling her six-stool counter "Love Burgers" and sold her grease-splattered concoctions for twenty-five cents, or a dime, or nothing, if you were really hungry. On holidays, the burgers were always free and people lined up for blocks to get them. She housed unwed mothers and held Easter Egg hunts, but outsiders like Graham simply saw the sign and assumed it was another sleazy rip-off. Alas, "Love Burgers" is no more, although the Pall Mall itself continues as it did before, during, and after the height of the Haight.

The Psychedelic Shop
1535 Haight Street

The daringly named head store opened January 3, 1966, owned by brothers Jay and Ron Thelin, natives of the neighborhood whose father once managed the Woolworth's across the street. The brothers—psychedelic seekers who thought a store that pulled together in one place literature, records, incense, posters and, of course, tickets to rock concerts, was just what the Haight needed—may not have originally envisioned their store as the street's primary hangout, but it soon became exactly that. In fact, when the Straight Theater ripped out the old theater seats to make way for a dance floor and placed them on the sidewalk outside to give away, the Thelins promptly installed a pair in the store's window so people could sit and watch the parade go by. The most celebrated incident in the store's colorful history took place in October 1967, when police burst into the shop, seized copies of an obscure book of poetry titled *The Love Book* by an equally obscure Lenore Kandel, and arrested *Oracle* editor Allen Cohen, who happened to be working the cash register that day, on charges of selling obscene literature. The book had sold some fifty copies prior to the bust. Afterward, sales went through the ceiling and Kandel eventually announced she would donate one percent of her royalties to the police retirement fund as a way of saying thanks. Sometime the next year, the Thelins' answer to the unrest on Haight was to set aside half the store as a meditation room called the Calm Center.

George Hunter Apartment
200 Downey Street

A former architectural model maker fascinated with rock bands since discovering the Rolling Stones, George Hunter actually began designing his own rock group at a drafting table in his apartment in early 1965. He envisioned a group that encompassed his obsessions with Victoriana and the Wild West (an avid collector of antiques, Hunter stocked his apartment like a museum). He recruited some members, and the band held rehearsals daily at his apartment until, by chance, they landed an audition as house band at the Red Dog Saloon in Virginia City, Nevada, a Silver Rush dance hall being restored by some crazed hippies. At the band's first public performance, the group won the job and The Charlatans launched the acid-rock era of San Francisco music high in the Sierra Nevada. When the group returned triumphant to town, The Charlatans headlined the first Family Dog dance-concert at Longshoremen's Hall in October 1965.

Airplane Mansion
2400 Fulton Street

Based in a manor built at the turn of the century by a lumber baron said to have provided refuge to opera singer Enrico Caruso on the night of the 1906 earthquake, the Jefferson Airplane reigned as the uncrowned heads of state on the San Francisco rock scene in the late sixties. In May 1968, the band applied a $20,000 down payment toward a total purchase price of $70,000 and took possession of the enormous four-story mansion with a grand staircase and mahogany banister that had been shipped around Cape Horn. The place served as a combination office, rehearsal hall, and home to band members through the seventies, until the defunct group cashed in its real estate investment for a generous profit. But throughout their tenure here, the Airplane presided over much madness. One epic bash staged in September 1968, after the band returned from a European tour with the Doors, was immortalized on the cover of the live album, *Bless Its Pointed Little Head*, a title taken from a remark made by Grace Slick when she was shown the cover photo of bassist Jack Casady passed out, his hand still wrapped around a bottle.

The Blues Brothers repaired to the mansion following their performance at the final Winterland show, New Year's Eve 1979, for a party that truly rang out the decadent decade in a lavish, degenerate style. With the imposing black facade, the Airplane mansion served as a kind of underground landmark for many years. Then-Mayor Dianne Feinstein, invited to participate in a press conference, walked into the foyer with a surprised look on her face. "I always wondered who lived here," she said.

Airplane Mansion. (1995, photo by Keta Bill Selvin)

Haight-Ashbury

Pine Street Commune
1836 Pine Street

Light show artist Bill Ham managed these apartments for an absentee landlord and filled the premises with every woebegone miscreant he could find. With artists and musicians crammed into every available room, the place became a beehive of activity during the early days of the Fillmore/Avalon years. Ham perfected his nascent psychedelic light show each night in a basement room. He eventually mounted the show at the Avalon Ballroom. Some of The Charlatans lived there, as did some members of Big Brother and the Holding Company. These apartments were the first place Janis Joplin lived in San Francisco when she returned to town to join Big Brother.

Dog House
2125 Pine Street

When they were planning their original concert at Longshoremen's Hall, the members of the first acid-rock concert production troupe all lived at Dog House, so called because of the tenants' propensity for owning pet dogs and to commemorate the many who lost their lives to Pine Street rush hour. The Family Dog became the name for the members' concert production company.

Kelley-Mouse Studios
74 Henry Street

An old dairy, long ago torn down to make way for condominiums, that served as headquarters of prolific poster artists was where Big Brother and the Holding Company first met Janis Joplin in 1966. In town from Texas at the suggestion of Avalon Ballroom proprietor/band manager Chet Helms, Joplin showed up for rehearsal, her hair in a bun, her blouse knotted at her midriff. Nobody remembers being too impressed. Eventually, however, they were. Her practiced howl and startling vocal power, on at least one occasion, convinced neighbors that some poor woman was being assaulted. They summoned the police.

Janis Joplin Apartment
892 Noe Street

While Big Brother and the Holding Company were finishing the band's Columbia Records debut, *Cheap Thrills,* Janis Joplin and roommate Linda Gravenites hastily found this apartment, Joplin stashing boxes in the hallway before heading off for recording sessions in Los Angeles. She lived at this address from spring 1968 to December 1969, when she bought a spacious house in the woods of Marin County that was more suited to her new rock-star lifestyle. For most of the period she was quartered at the Noe Street apartment, she spent little time at home, touring, first, with Big Brother (whose album *Cheap Thrills* hit number one on the charts in November 1968) and, later, with her own band.

Kezar Stadium
Frederick and Stanyan streets

Built in 1924 and named for Mary Kezar, who left $100,000 in her will to the city for construction, the stadium served as the home of the San Francisco 49ers football team until 1970, when it was deserted except for the annual East-West Shrine game each fall. Producer Bill Graham inaugurated his "Day on the Green" series in May 1973 at the former football field with a bill featuring the Grateful Dead, New Riders of the Purple Sage, and, in his first performance at a rock concert, country singer Waylon Jennings. Asked if his noon set time was unusual, Jennings cracked a smile. "Hell, son," he said, "on the hillbilly circuit, they'll book you at seven in the morning for a chicken fight, if they can git ya." The following month, Graham brought Led Zeppelin to the Kezar for an epic performance, even if the band arrived two-and-a-half hours late. The Tubes opened the show, with lead vocalist Quay Lewd tossing giant styrofoam pills into the crowd and shoveling fake "cocaine" onto the front rows. In 1975, Graham returned to the Kezar for his mammoth SNACK concert to benefit after-school athletic programs, a one-day concert broadcast live on K101-FM and featuring Bob Dylan as the surprise guest with Neil Young, actor Marlon Brando, the Grateful Dead, Jefferson Starship, Joan Baez, Tower of Power, The Doobie Brothers, Santana, and others. The day after the benefit, an accounting error turned up the funds missing from the budget for the canceled programs anyway.

Kezar Pavilion
Frederick and Stanyan streets

The Clash stormed the former home of USF basketball and roller derby with one rock concert at the tile-roofed building on the edge of Golden Gate Park in October 1979. The band's second appearance in town more than compensated for the sorry show the British politico-punkers played the previous February at the Berkeley Community Theater, even if the performance was delayed for an hour while one of the musicians found his way to the hall.

Panhandle
Golden Gate Park, between Oak and Fell streets

This strip of green stretching beyond the park's entrance, just a few blocks north of the Haight, was the site of many impromptu free concerts during the height of the sixties scene. The Grateful Dead and Big Brother and the Holding Company played a notable concert near the Cole Street intersection on October 6, 1966, to celebrate the outlawing of LSD. Fugitive Ken Kesey made a clandestine appearance at the event and escaped before FBI agents could catch him. But the most famous free concert here occurred on a June weekend in 1967, when, with equipment borrowed from the Jefferson Airplane, the Jimi Hendrix Experience played.

Lindley Meadows
Golden Gate Park

Although billed as Jerry Garcia and Friends, the Grateful Dead returned from a year-long "retirement" in September 1975 to this sylvan glade for a free concert with the Jefferson Starship before a crowd of more than thirty-five thousand people. The Starship had played a free concert at the site the previous summer to a slightly smaller crowd and returned a couple of years later as the surprise guest on a radio station-sponsored event headlined by the Greg Kihn Band. The long, narrow corridor lined by trees made Lindley Meadows a particularly commodious setting for outdoor concerts.

Bandshell

Golden Gate Park

60   Despite the visual obstructions caused by the trees in the seating area, this old-fashioned bandstand between Steinhart Aquarium and the de Young Museum has been the scene of numerous free concerts over the years, including the annual Comedy Day marathon. The Kantner-Balin-Casady Band brought free music back to the park after a lengthy absence in a 1985 concert. The Jerry Garcia Band and an acoustic performance by Grace Slick and Paul Kantner, reunited after she left the Starship, celebrated the end of the 1988 U.S./U.S.S.R. Peace Walk here. In 1973, Todd Rundgren recorded vocal overdubs from the audience at the Bandshell while singing "Sons of 1984," which he mixed with a similar recording from New York's Wollman Rink. The result appeared on his album, *Todd*.

Polo Fields

Golden Gate Park

On January 14, 1967, "A Gathering of the Tribes—Human Be-In" attracted a crowd of one hundred thousand to hear Allen Ginsberg, Tim Leary, and Gary Snyder hold forth between rock bands like Jefferson Airplane, the Grateful Dead, Quicksilver Messenger Service, and Sir Douglas Quintet. Jazz flautist Charles Lloyd sat in with the Dead, and Hell's Angels served peacefully as security guards. Years later, more than three hundred thousand people filled the enormous playing field in October 1991 for "Laughter, Love and Music," the free memorial concert for Bill Graham the week after he died. Appearing on the daylong concert were Crosby, Stills, Nash and Young, the Grateful Dead, John Fogerty, a reunited Journey, Santana, Robin Williams, and Bobby McFerrin. Peter Gabriel appeared in a paid performance the following year, headlining his multicultural WOMAD Festival for the final date on its first U.S. tour before the largest crowd in the ten-year history of the moving festival. Pearl Jam canceled the band's remaining tour dates in June 1995 after vocalist Eddie Vedder, suffering from stomach flu, left the stage after six songs. Neil Young took over the show and played two hours with the remaining members of the band. The Polo Fields also served as the site of the public memorial service for Jerry Garcia in August 1995.

Crosby, Stills, Nash and Young play the Bill Graham memorial concert at the Polo Fields. (1991, photo by Scott Sommerdorf)

Haight-Ashbury

The Musical History Tour

3

1

2

Around Downtown

Enrico Caruso and the great earthquake ...
Billie Holiday drug bust ... Duke Ellington's
sacred concert ... Louis Armstrong's jam
session ... Thelonious Monk and Miles Davis ...
Nat King Cole and Sammy Davis Jr. ...
Bill Graham and Chet Helms ... the Airplane,
Dead, Santana, and Creedence in the studio ...
the humble beginnings of *Rolling Stone*
magazine ... Bob Dylan's gospel concerts ...
U2's free concert

1 Loew's Warfield
2 Billie Holliday
▼ Market Street

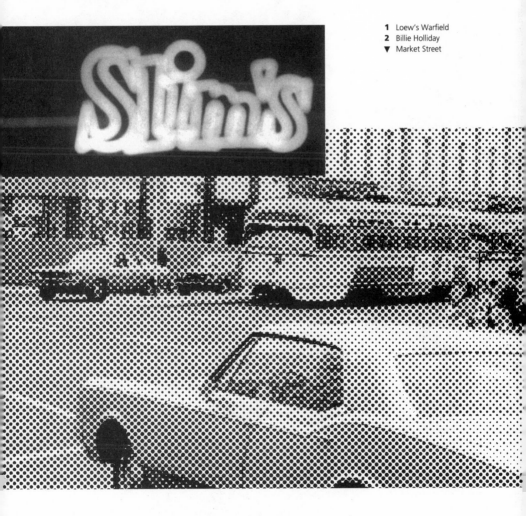

Around Downtown

1 Bill Graham Civic Auditorium	14 Slim's	31 Dawn Club
2 War Memorial Opera House	15 Blackhawk	32 Palace Hotel
3 Davies Symphony Hall	16 Wally Heider's Studios	33 Mars Hotel
4 Veterans' Building	17 Great American Music Hall	34 Wade's Opera House
5 Fillmore West	18 Mark Twain Hotel	35 The Automatt
6 Fillmore Records Office	19 Clift Hotel	36 Mime Troupe Loft
7 Tommy's Joynt	20 St. Francis Hotel	37 Rolling Stone Offices
8 California Hall	21 Grace Cathedral	38 Tin Angel
9 FM Productions	22 Masonic Auditorium	39 Old Waldorf
10 Avalon Ballroom	23 Venetian Room, Fairmont Hotel	40 Justin Herman Plaza
11 Hard Rock Cafe	24 Club Hangover	
12 Pacific High Studios	25 Say When	
13 Bill Graham Presents	26 Boarding House	
	27 Wentley Apartments	
	28 Mocombo	
	29 Orpheum Theater	
	30 Warfield Theater	

The Musical History Tour

Bill Graham Civic Auditorium
99 Grove Street, Civic Center Plaza

Renamed in 1992 following the concert promoter's death, the San Francisco Civic Auditorium, as it was known during his lifetime, was never Bill Graham's favorite place for a concert. The main auditorium in the seven thousand-seat arena was too boxy, too boomy, never really the right size except for a few attractions a year.

Built for the 1915 Panama Pacific Exposition, the San Francisco Exposition Hall, as it was first known, housed the enormous Austin pipe organ that composer Camille Saint-Saëns played during his visit to the world's fair. The Democratic National Convention of 1920 held at the Exposition Hall nominated a ticket featuring Ohio governor James Cox for president and a young former cabinet member for vice-president named Franklin D. Roosevelt.

Extensively remodeled in 1964 and closed in 1993 for seismic upgrades, the Civic has been used memorably over the years, not the least for the annual Bay Area Music Awards and Margot St. James's memorable Hookers' Balls during the seventies, but also for concerts by acts ranging from U2 to Bette Midler, John Denver to Prince. The Rolling Stones concert in 1965 at the Civic was something of a watershed event in the emerging local music scene; most of the musicians who played in bands at the Fillmore and Avalon the next year attended the show. The Black and White Balls have used the spacious room as a location for rock bands, featuring acts like the Neville Brothers and Boz Scaggs.

Bill Graham Civic Auditorium. (1953, photo by Joe Rosenthal)

Around Downtown

War Memorial Opera House

301 Van Ness Avenue

Opened in 1932, the building was designed by architect Arthur Brown Jr., creator of such San Francisco landmarks as City Hall and Coit Tower. The annual season by the world-renowned resident opera company has left little room in the hall's schedule for other musical events. Over the years some special pop music performances have taken place at the historic hall, where the final articles of surrender from World War II were signed by Japan and the charter for the United Nations was first ratified in 1945. Carole King played a serene concert at the sumptuous house at the height of her popularity and the Pointer Sisters recorded a live album in 1974, *Live at the Opera House*, before a tuxedo-clad audience a little more than a year after breaking their act in at the three hundred-seat Boarding House on nearby Bush Street. At the height of his disco success, Sylvester put on a remarkable live concert at the hall titled "Flowers While You Live." In 1982, dying of cancer at age thirty-three, *San Francisco Chronicle* jazz critic Conrad Silvert assembled an extraordinary lineup of jazz greats, including Herbie Hancock, Wynton Marsalis, Wayne Shorter, Sonny Rollins, Tony Williams, Charlie Haden, Denny Zeitlin, Toshiko Akiyoshi, Bobby Hutcherson, and others, that was recorded for a Columbia Records album, *Conrad Silvert Presents Jazz at the Opera House*. In 1994, the San Francisco engagement of the Broadway musical version of *The Who's Tommy* played for six weeks at the venerable old hall one year before undergoing some $40 million worth of structural repairs and seismic upgrades following the 1989 earthquake.

War Memorial Opera House. (1949, photo by Bob Campbell)

Davies Symphony Hall
Grove and Van Ness avenues

As with the Opera House, the rigorous schedule of San Francisco Symphony events has precluded many other concerts from taking place here. Originally opened in 1980 and renovated in 1991, the hall has almost exclusively been used for classical music, although, in typical San Francisco fashion, some concerts have included collaborations with such pop-culture escapees as Bobby McFerrin, Robin Williams, and Linda Ronstadt. In 1982, Joan Baez and Paul Simon performed a solo acoustic concert together here and Werner Erhard's EST managed to put together a 1981 program that included John Denver, Paul Williams, Connie Stevens, and Phyllis Diller.

Veterans' Building
Van Ness and MacAllister streets

In spring 1943, jazz historian Rudi Blesh gave a series of lectures here (at the former home of the Museum of Modern Art) that prompted one of the most remarkable comebacks in the history of jazz. Cornetist Bunk Johnson, who played with the legendary Buddy Bolden at the very beginnings of the music, had been corresponding with jazz historians for many years from his home in the Tabasco town of New Iberia, Louisiana, where he worked an assortment of odd jobs but had grown remote from any connection with the music business. A collection was taken among traditional-jazz enthusiasts across the country and a new horn and a new set of false teeth were purchased for Johnson. After a couple of brief, experimental sessions in New Orleans, Johnson came to San Francisco by train to appear at the Blesh lecture series, where he played cornet, accompanied by local pianist Bertha Gonsoulin (who had played with King Oliver). Johnson told his own story, and told the crowd, "I am as honored to be with you as I know you are to have me." He stayed in San Francisco for the next couple of years, playing a concert at the Geary Theater with fellow Dixielanders Kid Ory and Mutt Carey, leading his own band at the CIO Hall, and making a few recordings before returning to New Iberia. The next year he was playing in New York, contemplating a film offer, cutting sessions with another New Orleans jazz great, Sidney Bechet, performing in clubs, concerts, jam sessions, and on radio, and was written up in *Time, Vogue, The New Yorker,* and other magazines. He died after a stroke in 1949 at age seventy back home in New Iberia, after a rediscovery he never could have imagined was possible.

Fillmore West

Market Street and Van Ness Avenue

All the big bands of the thirties and forties passed through the Carousel Ballroom, then known as the El Patio, but the painted lady had lost her youthful good looks by the time Grateful Dead associate Ron Rakow ran across the upstairs ballroom. Backed by a partnership that included the Dead, Jefferson Airplane, and Quicksilver Messenger Service, Rakow operated the Carousel for six months in 1968 with the renegade menace of a hippie freak who was part con man, part visionary. He once let the Hell's Angels put on a bail fundraiser where they gave away free beer. So much suds was spilled that the carpet squished when people walked on it and the lighting fixtures in the rug store downstairs filled with beer. That little episode drew a phalanx of armed police from the Tactical Squad waiting down the street to quell any potential disturbance. The Free City Convention, an authentic free-for-all happening that lasted all night and into the morning, was an even more uncontrolled event. Admission was either by buying a ticket at the box office—one fellow threw a bloody leg of lamb across the counter as barter—or by going through the back door and tossing money in a bonfire.

A crowd waits outside the Fillmore West for one of the final week's concerts. (1971, photographer unknown)

The Musical History Tour

Obviously, such an enterprise was not destined to last, even though some extraordinary shows took place at the hall under Rakow's sponsorship (Thelonious Monk, Dr. John the Nighttripper, and The Charlatans were on the same bill, for instance). Eventually, Bill Graham negotiated the lease out from under Rakow and moved his Fillmore Auditorium operation to Fillmore West, as he renamed the hall, over the Fourth of July weekend, 1968. Until he closed the enterprise in June 1971, Graham ran shows every weekend at the hall, some, like the final appearance of Janis Joplin with Big Brother and the Holding Company, that were so crowded that people were literally gasping for breath on the fire escapes.

The Who put on some amazing performances of *Tommy* there and Aretha Franklin, backed by the King Curtis Band (with Billy Preston on organ), blew the place into the Bay and came back for an encore with Ray Charles on her arm, all recorded for a live album. Johnny Winter took the Fillmore West stage for a highly anticipated appearance following the hubbub surrounding his first album, only to find himself upstaged by a cunning veteran, guitarist Lonnie Mack. Eric Clapton played his final shows as lead guitarist with Delaney and Bonnie. Al Kooper and Mike Bloomfield took over the room to cut the follow-up to their million-selling *Super Session* album, *The Live Adventures of Al Kooper and Mike Bloomfield.* When Bloomfield fell ill and canceled his second-night performance, Kooper substituted Elvin Bishop and a young unknown guitarist making his recording debut, Carlos Santana. Bloomfield later recorded a number of live albums at the hall with various groups, including one loose association of talent (including Taj Mahal) simply titled *Live at Bill Graham's Fillmore West.* The band Santana consistently headlined the hall long before it released its first album.

The final week at the Fillmore West built up over six days, and featured virtually every major act from town, live broadcasts on the radio, a deluxe boxed-set recording, and a movie, *Fillmore: The Last Days.* The final night featured Tower of Power, Creedence Clearwater (appearing as a trio after the departure of rhythm guitarist Tom Fogerty, his brother John made over in a turquoise shirt and Elvis hairdo), and Santana, in what turned out to be the final appearance by the band's most popular lineup. The group offered its own version of a requiem, a cover of Joe Zawinul's "In a Silent Way," a number the band never performed before or since. A sprawling jam session followed, with an endless procession of players crowded onto the stage until the early morning hours: Mike Bloomfield, Van Morrison, Vince Guaraldi, and John Cipollina, among dozens of others.

Around Downtown

Fillmore Records Office
1550 Market Street

Across the street from Fillmore West, Bill Graham maintained a third-floor office from which he launched his record labels, Fillmore Records and San Francisco Records, in 1969. Fillmore Records producers Jeffrey Cohen and Bruce Good once brought Rod Stewart across the street after a Small Faces show at the Fillmore West and pitched Stewart on signing with Fillmore as a solo artist. Graham's partner and staff producer for the labels, David Rubinson, continued to work out of offices on the second floor of the building after he split with Graham, where he managed and produced acts such as the Pointer Sisters and Herbie Hancock.

Tommy's Joynt
Geary Street at Van Ness Avenue

After auditioning a few dozen candidates to replace bassist Cliff Burton, who died in a bus crash on a Swedish tour in September 1986, the three remaining members of Metallica took Phoenix-based Jason Newsted of Flotsam and Jetsam to have a bite to eat at this long-established San Francisco hof brau (famous for its buffalo stew) and asked him to join the band. Among those also auditioning for the job was Metallica guitarist Kirk Hammett's high school buddy, Les Claypool, who later formed his own band, Primus.

Tommy's Joynt, where Metallica added a new bassist. (1995, photo by Keta Bill Selvin)

California Hall

625 Polk Street

Now home to the California Culinary Academy, California Hall hosted two dances thrown by the Family Dog in late 1965, before Chet Helms took over the name and moved operations to the Avalon. The Charlatans played a signal event at the hall the same night Ken Kesey and the Merry Pranksters threw one of their public bacchanals they called an Acid Test at the Fillmore Auditorium. A bus ran between the two locations.

Modeled after a Heidelberg castle and opened in 1912 with royal best wishes from Kaiser Wilhelm, Das Deutsches Haus changed its named to the more patriotic California Hall at the start of World War I. More than forty-three German societies and lodges used the hall when it first opened and it is said that bund meetings took place in the hall before World War II.

Over the years, occasional concerts took place at the hall, like punk and reggae, but shows didn't catch on here. The basement restaurant, the Rathskeller, gained a little notoriety as the scene of a scandalous off-duty police initiation ceremony involving a blindfolded rookie and a prostitute during the seventies. The officially recognized landmark building was sold in 1983 for more than $3 million by the descendants of the original investors.

FM Productions

675 Golden Gate Avenue

Big Brother and the Holding Company used this warehouse as a rehearsal hall before and after Janis Joplin left the band in 1969. Under the baton of guitarist Mike Bloomfield, Joplin also threw together her first solo band in a hasty three-day session before making a disastrous debut at Memphis's Stax/Volt Christmas concert in 1968. Big Brother guitarist James Gurley lived in the hall when the band wasn't trying out new vocalists and contemplating what to do in the wake of their vocalist and main meal ticket. Soon after, Bill Graham rented the place as offices for his expanding operation. Only a few short blocks from his Fillmore West offices, Graham at first ran the FM Productions arm of his business out of the Golden Gate Avenue warehouse. But after he closed Fillmore West in 1971, he moved his entire company into these informal surroundings.

Avalon Ballroom
1268 Sutter Street

Small bits of the original decorations remain in the Regency II movie theater from its days as one of the cradles of San Francisco rock, the Avalon Ballroom. It was at the Avalon in June 1966 that Janis Joplin made her first public performance as vocalist with Big Brother and the Holding Company. A few months before, beginning in April 1966 with a bill featuring the Blues Project and the Great Society, the Family Dog, under the direction of Chet Helms, presented a series of shows through November 1968. Helms ran the dance hall most favored by authentic hippies; the Avalon was the real deal.

Helms, in many ways, stayed closer to the grassroots community than his competitor Bill Graham and, as a result, was able to ferret out some ascending bands, like Moby Grape or Steve Miller Blues Band. Country Joe and the Fish was Helms's typical New Year's Eve headliner and he loved to dabble in old rock-and-roll acts like Bill Haley and his Comets or Bo Diddley, whose double bill with Big Brother and the Holding Company was one of the highlights of his two-and-a-half years at the Avalon.

Built in 1911 and called the Puckett Academy of Dance, the upstairs ballroom featured a wood dance floor, an L-shaped balcony, and mirrors, columns, gilded booths, and red-flocked wallpaper when Helms took over and replaced the Irish dances. With promotional psychedelic concert posters spreading the name around the world, the Avalon Ballroom has become a spot most identified with those heady days of San Francisco rock.

Helms lost his permits after much-exaggerated complaints about noise. Another production company, ironically named Soundproof Productions, tried to throw shows at the hall the following year, but the room had been vacant for ages when it was finally converted into a cineplex during the seventies.

Hard Rock Cafe
1699 Van Ness Avenue

Amid all the regulation Hard Rock memorabilia, the "San Francisco Wall of Fame" makes an uncharacteristic concession to the city's psychedelic rock past with an assortment of Fillmore and Avalon posters, as well as guitars from Sammy Hagar, Joe Satriani, Todd Rundgren, Counting Crows, and Faith No More to further localize its already impressive collection. An enormous Elvis billboard for *Jailhouse Rock* sits above the kitchen and another entire wall is covered with Elvis's gold records surrounding a framed cape from his Las Vegas years. M.C. Hammer's glittery suit from one of his videos is in a glass case outside the bathrooms.

The free New Year's Eve shows here have always featured stellar attractions—the Counting Crows appeared mere weeks before the band's debut album broke big-time—and the restaurant has been the site of the occasional radio-station promotion. With "Girls Just Want to Have Fun" steaming up the charts, Cyndi Lauper appeared at the charity opener in 1984, the night before her big Bay Area concert debut, and she drew such a huge crowd, even at seventy-five bucks a throw, that latecomers had to watch her performance on video from the parking garage upstairs. Security guards at first kept Deborah Iyall of Romeo Void standing outside on the sidewalk before saner minds finally prevailed and she wound up singing background vocals on Lauper's hit that night onstage.

Pacific High Studios
60 Brady Street

Close to Fillmore West, the city's first twelve-track recording studio was where the Grateful Dead recorded *Workingman's Dead* in nine days in 1969. With Richard Olsen of The Charlatans acting as studio manager, most of the local bands tried out the studio—Steve Miller, Quicksilver Messenger Service, It's a Beautiful Day, and Van Morrison. KSAN used the studio as the location for some early live broadcasts. The Dead's engineers took over the place briefly in the seventies, under the name Alembic Studios, before Neil Young producer Elliott Mazer (*Harvest*) bought the studio and renamed it His Master's Wheels. During sessions for the Journey album *Infinity*, producer Roy Thomas Baker, famous for the majestic sound of the Queen albums, blew off some steam by spraying the studio and everyone in it with a chemical fire extinguisher. As the fog settled on Mazer's expensive recording equipment, the corrosive chemicals covered the console in a sizzling, bubbling ooze. Mazer was summoned, angry words were spoken, and in the late midnight hour at the studio, blows may have been exchanged. But, suffice it to say, Baker never returned to the studio and Journey finished the album somewhere else.

Bill Graham Presents
201 Eleventh Street

This large corner building housed the entire Graham operation from 1972 to 1985, when it was destroyed by a firebomb. Graham had taken out full-page newspaper ads deploring President Reagan's visit to the Bitburg Cemetery in Germany, where members of the S.S. lay buried, and although arson inspectors never made any arrests or found any suspects, the fire seemed a little too coincidental not to mean something. Graham himself always considered the bombing an act of anti-Semitic terrorism.

Slim's
333 Eleventh Street

When Boz Scaggs decided to open a nightclub in the suddenly fashionable nightclub strip growing along South of Market's Eleventh Street, he leased an old restaurant called The Warehouse, previously owned by the folks who pioneered the neighborhood across the street at another club, the Oasis. Scaggs played a jam session to christen the joint on New Year's Eve 1987. But the work of turning the bare shell of the room into a proper nightclub soon slowed as expenses mounted and Scaggs took on new partners, including Bob Brown, manager of Huey Lewis and the News.

Huey Lewis manager and Slim's co-owner Bob Brown. (1988, photo by Brant Ward)

When the club finally opened in September 1988, the plan called for Slim's to be primarily a rhythm and blues club (Johnnie Taylor was one of the club's first attractions), but filling a monthly booking calendar without ranging far and wide into the realm of contemporary pop music soon proved impossible for Slim's bookers. While retaining a substantial lineup of r&b acts, the club delved into the local alternative rock scene, presented lots of world beat and jazz, rock, folk, country, and actually, anything.

Pearl Jam played a surprise date at the club while living in the area recording *Vs.* The Black Crowes chose Slim's as the location for the band's "secret" club tour promoting the release of *Amorica* in 1994. David Bowie played the club with his band Tin Machine during a record-industry convention.

Laurie Anderson and Rickie Lee Jones have played the six hundred-seat room. Huey Lewis and the News have made several appearances at the club (but, then, club management does have a direct line to the band). Was/Not Was developed a substantial following in San Francisco, thanks to the club's belief in the zany act. Likewise, surf guitar king Dick Dale played practically the first dates of his career outside of Southern California at the club, leading directly to his rediscovery and first new records in decades. Sun Ra and his Arkestra played the club every Halloween until his death. Mary Chapin-Carpenter was in the middle of a set when a power outage hit the block. She grabbed an accordion, stood on the bar in the middle of the room, and continued her performance.

Among the people who have recorded live albums at the popular nightspot are Joe Louis Walker, Irma Thomas, and American Music Club. P.J. Harvey shot one of her videos there. And, yes, owner Scaggs can be found from time to time sitting in with whoever's playing.

Blackhawk

200 Hyde Street

An empty lot marks the site of one of the country's most celebrated jazz clubs, although the Blackhawk itself has been closed since 1963. But for fourteen years, the best and the brightest in the world of jazz passed through those portals. Dave Brubeck, Shorty Rogers, Gerry Mulligan, and Cal Tjader used the club as a springboard. Billie Holiday and Lester Young played their last West Coast club dates here and the Modern Jazz Quartet played its first. Miles Davis, Thelonious Monk, Shelley Manne, Tjader, and Brubeck all recorded albums at the club. When Charlie Parker was supposed to be opening across town at the Say When, he could be found instead jamming at the 'Hawk.

"I've worked and slaved for years to keep this place a sewer," boasted owner Guido Caccienti, who, with boyhood chum Johnny Noga, scraped together

Special seating section for minors at the Blackhawk, a brief cause célèbre. (1961, photo by Gordon Peters)

77

$10,000 and bought the old Stork Club at a sheriff's auction in 1949. They booked a band featuring Noga's younger brother, the Eastmen Trio, followed by a couple of other square attractions like the Pied Pipers. Caccienti's wife, Elynore, worked the cash register at the front door. Noga married the cocktail waitress, Helen, and the two men did the bartending.

In 1950, jazz disc jockey Jimmy Lyons was playing the first records by a local musician named Dave Brubeck and suggested booking the group. The first night, the Dave Brubeck Trio (featuring Cal Tjader on drums) drew so poorly that Caccienti put them on notice. But Brubeck did catch on. The Red Norvo Trio with Charlie Mingus on bass and Tal Farlow on guitar followed the suddenly ascendant Brubeck group and the club was launched.

In 1953 alone, the club presented Anita O'Day, the Gerry Mulligan Quartet (with Chet Baker), Erroll Garner, and Oscar Peterson. In 1955, the 'Hawk introduced the historic Chico Hamilton Quartet. When glamorous actress Dorothy Dandridge showed up for her engagement, with arrangements for a fifteen-piece band and trunks of costumes, asking for the dressing room, Caccienti—who expected a female piano player named Dorothy Donegan—showed her the space behind the refrigerator in the rear of the club.

After signing Johnny Mathis to a personal-manager contract, Helen Noga and her husband sold their interest in the club to George and Max Weiss, owners of Fantasy Records. In 1961, the club became a minor cause célèbre when Mayor George Christopher noticed the 'Hawk maintained a section reserved for underage patrons and ordered it closed. He faced outrage on all fronts and, eventually, reversed his decision.

Caccienti, in whose mangled English saxophonist Illinois Jacquet became Indiana Jacket, closed the club for good in 1963. The place was a dump. Pigeons roosted in the ceiling, dirty glasses and foul air added to the ambience. But the jazz world loved the joint. On closing night, with Cal Tjader at the bandstand and visiting firemen like John Handy and Vince Guaraldi sitting in, Tjader made a teary, sentimental speech announcing the final number. "I just can't believe that we won't be back on Tuesday night," he said.

Wally Heider's Studios
245 Hyde Street

When Wally Heider opened his San Francisco studio in April 1969, he brought the science of modern recording to this provincial outpost. Heider, one of the industry's top recordists, ran one of Hollywood's favorite studios and his investment in the burgeoning San Francisco music scene represented an unprecedented endorsement from the supposedly entrenched industry of Southern California. Immediately, Crosby, Stills, Nash and Young took over the studio to record their second album, *Deja Vu.* Crosby spent endless months putting together his solo album with members of the Grateful Dead, Santana, and Jefferson Airplane. The Airplane recorded *Volunteers* at the studio. The Dead made *American Beauty,* and Santana cut *Abraxas* here. Derek and the Dominos, in fact, visited the *Abraxas* sessions, resulting in an all-night jam session. And, starting with *Green River,* Creedence Clearwater began recording all their records at the Tenderloin studio. Heider was off to a good start for his first year in business in San Francisco. The studio has changed hands many times since Heider retired in the seventies, but continues to hold sessions.

Great American Music Hall
859 O'Farrell Street

Built in 1907 and initially operated as a fancy French restaurant and bordello called Blanco's, and occupied during the thirties by famed stripper Sally Rand, the Great American Music Hall still sports the baroque gilded interior suited to its original purpose. Since 1972, however, the room has been one of the cornerstones of the San Francisco nightclub scene. Jazz fan Tom Bradshaw opened the club as a haven for the genre, at that time something of an endangered species in the nightlife world, and all the greats, from royalty like Duke Ellington and Count Basie on down, paraded across the stage. The very first act Bradshaw booked was guitarists Herb Ellis and Joe Pass. Over the years, however, Bradshaw and his wife, Jeannie, gradually transformed the club's booking policy into a potpourri of contemporary music, namely jazz, folk, rock, and comedy. Van Morrison has a particular love affair with the club, leftover from his days living in Marin County when he would call Bradshaw and arrange dates, often with no more than twenty-four hours notice.

Robin Williams filmed his famous Home Box Office special at the club. The Grateful Dead rigged up the band's sophisticated sound system for a special performance for radio programmers in 1975, in town for a convention, piping the sound of live crickets from the basement into the quadrophonic mix. The event previewed the band's *Blues for Allah* album in a performance later released as the first in a series of live recordings from the Dead's tape vault. Betty Carter and Carmen MacRae recorded a live album of duets for the club's own label in 1987. The club teamed French jazz violinist Stephane Grapelli with Django-inspired Marin mandolinist David Grisman. British pop song-smith Alan Price brought a full string section with him for one of three U.S. dates in 1974. John Lee Hooker was joined by Bonnie Raitt, Robert Cray, Carlos Santana, Ry Cooder, and others for his 1990 special. Billy Joel and k.d. lang made early career appearances at the club.

In 1991, the Bradshaws, no longer married but still amicably operating the Music Hall together, sold the club to a group of investors headed by venture capitalist/author Kurt Brouwer, who has slowly seen to much of the deferred maintenance leftover from the Bradshaw years. The Mitchell Brothers, next-door neighbors, saw to the club's cinematic immortalization by using the room to stage the climactic orgy scene to their follow-up to *Behind the Green Door,* another Marilyn Chambers vehicle titled *The Resurrection of Eve.*

Mark Twain Hotel
345 Taylor Street

Police broke down the door of room 203 in January 1949 in time to grab jazz vocal great Billie Holiday, in town playing an engagement at Cafe Society, in the bathroom just before she flushed a small package and its contents. She and a friend, John Levy, were arrested on charges of opium possession, a second drug offense for Holiday, who had been arrested and convicted on drug charges two years before in Philadelphia. By the time her trial was over, famed defense attorney Jake Erlich had fingered Levy as an informer and con-vinced a jury to return a verdict of not guilty. In a typically San Francisco bit of perversity, the hotel now celebrates the incident by renting the historic room as the Billie Holiday Suite, decorated with newspaper clippings of the arrest. (But don't look for a Fatty Arbuckle Suite at the St. Francis.)

Clift Hotel

Geary and Taylor streets

The richly paneled Redwood Room off the lobby of the grand old hotel has gone from throwing out anyone with hair over their collar in the sixties—including Burt Lancaster's son, who dropped by with his dad for a drink—to hosting singalongs by crew and cast of the 1983 ARMS Concerts at the Cow Palace, Joe Cocker warbling away at the piano bench, with Chris Stainton accompanying him.

St. Francis Hotel

335 Powell Street

In October 1950, fatigued from an arduous tour of the Korean front entertaining the troops, Al Jolson nevertheless flew to San Francisco to tape a radio program with Bing Crosby. After a dinner of clam chowder and prawns at Fisherman's Wharf, Jolson and a pair of buddies retired to his suite at the St. Francis for a quiet round of gin rummy. When Jolson dropped his cards on the table and his eyes glazed over, a doctor was summoned. "You know, doc," he told the physician, "MacArthur only got one hour with Truman. I got two." With that, he died. The city where it started for the self-styled world's greatest entertainer almost forty-five years before at nickel-vaudeville theaters like the Globe Theater was where it all ended, in a hotel where radio programmers from all over the country assemble for the annual Gavin Conference, a convention of radio programmers, without the slightest hint of the hotel's connection to the century's first great pop singer. It was also at the St. Francis, around World War I, where drummer Art Hickman and pianist Ferde Grofé developed the basic concepts that became the first big band jazz arrangements.

Grace Cathedral

Taylor and California streets

As part of the Episcopal landmark's yearlong consecration celebration in 1965, Duke Ellington was commissioned to write a liturgical work. Ellington and his orchestra, augmented for the occasion by the Grace Cathedral Choir, the Herman McCoy Choir, singers Jon Hendricks, Esther Marrow, and Jimmy McPhail, and tap dancer Bunny Briggs, premiered his *Concert of Sacred Music* in the cathedral on September 16. Pianist Vince Guaraldi also recorded a lesser-known jazz mass at the cathedral later that same year. In 1972, engineer-producer Roy Halee took Art Garfunkel into the spacious sonic environment to record his first solo album, *Angel Clare*.

Masonic Auditorium
1111 California Street

Streisand played here and so did Sinatra. Dylan performed an oft-boot-legged concert in November 1964 at the Nob Hill temple, which first opened in 1958. Sitar master Ravi Shankar also recorded a live album at the Grand Lodge, as it is sometimes called. Groucho Marx gave the last concerts of his career here in 1972. Thelonious Monk, too, gave his final San Francisco performance at the room in 1973 with the "Giants of Jazz," a group that also included Dizzy Gillespie, Sonny Stitt, Art Blakey, and others. Van Morrison recorded his live album, *A Night in San Francisco*, during a 1992 run at the thirty-two hundred-seat hall.

Venetian Room
Fairmont Hotel, California and Mason streets

The last elegant supper club on the West Coast, this gilt-edged room decorated with murals was the first place Tony Bennett sang "I Left My Heart in San Francisco" in public. Opened in 1947, the biggest names in show business played during the forty-two years the room operated. Sammy Davis Jr., Lena Horne, Marlene Dietrich, Edith Piaf, and Louis Armstrong made appearances. Dean Martin and Jerry Lewis were fired after two days in 1955. When the Williams Brothers opened for Kay Thompson, young Andy Williams did little more than sing harmony and dance some soft shoe. The Swig family, owners of the hotel, were always progressive and booked many black acts who were making their first appearance in a major white nightclub: Will Mastin Trio (with a young Sammy Davis Jr.), Nat King Cole, Lou Rawls, even James Brown and Tina Turner. Ella Fitzgerald, practically an annual event at the room for decades, celebrated her sixty-fifth birthday here. "I can't imagine not playing there," she told a reporter. "It's not by any means a major source of income, but it feels like home. It's small, you're close to your audience, and you feel you're really in a very nice place, friendly, like a living room."

Also at the Fairmont, after World War I, a young viola player from the S.F. Symphony started his first orchestra in a room called Rainbow Lane. Paul Whiteman went on to become the most popular bandleader of the twenties and discovered such artists as singer Bing Crosby and cornetist Bix Beiderbecke.

Club Hangover
729 Bush Street

Doc Dougherty's Dixieland jazz headquarters throughout the fifties—where Muggsy Spanier played frequently, spelled by the likes of Wild Bill Davison, Jess Stacy, and Jimmy Rushing—hosted one of the great jam sessions in the annals of jazz. In January 1951, after visiting his old compadre, clarinetist Pee Wee Russell, near death in the charity ward of S.F. County Hospital, Louis Armstrong decided to raise some money for the pioneer jazzman. He brought together Earl "Fatha" Hines, Jack Teagarden, Barney Bigard, Cozy Cole, and Arvell Shaw at the club. Boogie-woogie piano great Meade "Lux" Lewis and a dozen others joined the festivities. The place was packed and some $1,500 went into the kitty that night. But old-timers still remember Armstrong and company wailing their way through "Royal Garden Blues," "Back of Town Blues," "Muskrat Ramble," "High Society," and "Way Down Yonder in New Orleans."

Say When
952 Bush Street

Another jumping jazz joint on the side of Nob Hill, the Say When veered from the hard-driving bebop of Charlie Parker to the frothy pop vocals of Ella Mae Morse. When Parker played the club, he fired his band after the first night and broke in a new one the next. Trumpeter Chet Baker, a private in the Sixth Army stationed at the Presidio, got his first real jazz gig that week with Parker's band at the club. Harry (The Hipster) Gibson, appearing at the club with Big Jay McNeely in the fifties, once grabbed a saxophone and began a wild solo as he walked out the door, got onboard a bus, and headed downtown. He returned by cab, still wailing away, and returned to the bandstand without dropping a stitch. A relic of San Francisco's post-war nightclub era, the Say When didn't last into the sixties.

Boarding House
960 Bush Street

David Allen ran, without doubt, the finest nightclub in San Francisco of the rock era, even though he never made a dime out of the perennially strapped enterprise. The three-hundred-and-thirty-pound entrepreneur could charm a PG&E bill collector into not only keeping the juice flowing but even offering Allen a small loan. Business was never his strong suit; talent was.

Boarding House owner David Allen, a great eye for talent. (1980, photo by Mike Maloney)

He knew Steve Martin could be a headliner, and booked Martin for two weeks in 1974, betting that word-of-mouth would sell out the second week. He was right and Martin's career was launched. Martin returned to the scene of the crime in 1977 to record his debut album, *Let's Get Small*. Allen saw Bette Midler coming a mile away. And he took a flier on a camped-up quartet of untried background singers testing the waters on their own, preacher's kids from Oakland called the Pointer Sisters, and had the place packed wall-to-wall.

Comedians making S.F. debuts at the Boarding House included Robert Klein, Lily Tomlin (who returned to play for Allen as long as he was in the business), Albert Brooks, Billy Crystal, Martin Mull, Gabe Kaplan, George Carlin, and Robin Williams. But he also brought rock music to the three hundred-seat club—Patti Smith, George Thorogood, the Talking Heads—along with acts like Manhattan Transfer, Willie Nelson, and Waylon Jennings. Allen introduced them all to San Francisco.

Emmylou Harris and the Hot Band, featuring James Burton on guitar and Glen D. Hardin of The Crickets on piano, made their public debut at the club in 1975. Bob Marley and the Wailers rocked the place to the rafters that same year for six nights. Neil Young tested a good deal of the material that eventually became *Rust Never Sleeps* during a 1978 five-night solo engagement at the club.

Not all the acts were successes. Barry Manilow played the club the very week his first hit, "Mandy," was number one on the charts in 1974, but had to cancel most of his late shows because of lack of interest.

The Musical History Tour

The room itself had boasted a checkered past. It was the Balalaika and the Hawaiian Gardens before the Andros brothers moved their Market Street operation to Nob Hill in 1956 and called the place Fack's II. Mel Torme opened the club and the Hi-Lo's played there, as did Lambert, Hendricks and Ross, and June Christy. Duke Ellington was scheduled to play a ten-day engagement in 1960 when the I.R.S. slapped a padlock on the joint, complaining about a measly $36,000 in unpaid taxes. The Neve opened that fall and the quality of bookings ran high—Ellington, Basie, Goodman, Woody Herman—but closed in less than a year. The Cellar featured topless waitresses serving lunch and the Quake mingled topless with facsimile earthquakes every hour. Coast Recorders operated the room as a recording studio for a while, but it was Doug Weston, who owned the Hollywood folk and rock institution, the Troubadour, whose Troubadour North on the premises in 1970 led to Allen taking over the site. Weston played acts like Elton John and Kris Kristofferson.

Allen, who once ran a shooting gallery on the top floor of California Hall and hosted a children's cartoon TV show in the fifties as Deputy Dave, worked as manager of the hungry i but parted ways with Enrico Banducci after Banducci closed the Jackson Street club and moved his operation to Ghirardelli Square. Allen then worked for Weston as manager of his new venture in San Francisco, then assumed the lease in 1972 and began booking six-night runs in a comfortable setting, with dinners served in a downstairs restaurant that never, ever made money. "I just got one of those pocket calculators for Christmas," Allen once explained, "and they are just amazing. I just discovered, for instance, that my kitchen consumes 105 percent of my gross. Aren't these calculators something?"

In fact, a loosely affiliated group calling themselves "Friends of the Boarding House" decided to raise enough money for Allen to buy a liquor license (he was probably the last nightclub owner in Western civilization to run a club serving only beer and wine). Steve Martin, Melissa Manchester, Jimmy Buffett, Joan Baez, Martin Mull, Billy Crystal, Loudon Wainwright III, and a newcomer fresh from a reprised version of TV's *Laugh-In,* Robin Williams, packed the S.F. Civic Auditorium in May 1978 and pitched $50,000 Allen's way.

How he managed to stay in business as long as he did is a tribute to his extraordinary feel for talent (he held monthly open auditions and took notes in Mandarin Chinese to discourage people from looking over his shoulder). But, when the end came, it was real estate developers who did him in, sending Allen and his toy train collection that decorated the downstairs bar out looking for a new location he could ill afford in May 1980. The club was subsequently torn down to make way for condominiums.

Around Downtown

Wentley Apartments
1214 Polk Street

Allen Ginsberg came to San Francisco in 1953 to visit an old lover, Neal Cassady, and stayed. He was living in a small apartment on the side of Nob Hill when, in a peyote-amphetamine swirl one weekend, he wrote much of what became the first section of the epic poem of the Beat generation, *Howl.* He finished the second section months later virtually in one sitting in the cafeteria at the Sir Francis Drake Hotel on Powell Street, having walked downtown muttering "Moloch, Moloch," after a vision of a robotic skullface he saw staring down into his apartment window from the top of the hotel's tower.

Mocombo
103 Powell Street

During his August 1956 engagement at this downtown jazz spot, Louis Jordan played "Caldonia" on a live telecast during *The Steve Allen Show* from the cable car turnaround down the street. The entire band boarded a cable car and rode off honking and squealing. By the sixties, however, this jazz club had descended into the seamy depths of clip joints with B-girls, shady ownership with possible mob connections—not to be confused with the rather elegant Polk Street club of the same name that opened in 1977 and catered to the gay trade with cabaret attractions like Eartha Kitt and Sally Kellerman.

Orpheum Theater
1192 Market Street

The original Orpheum Theater on O'Farrell Street (opposite Macy's) inaugurated the entire Orpheum circuit in vaudeville's heyday. George M. Cohan, Lew Dockstader, Lillian Russell, Eddie Cantor, George Jessel, Sophie Tucker, Harry Houdini—they all played the Orpheum. French actress Sarah Bernhardt made several appearances and Ruth St. Denis, the high priestess of modern dance, appeared on Orpheum bills between hoofers and jugglers. Moving to the Market Street location in 1926, the theater dumped vaudeville three years later and spent the next fifty years just running movies. In 1977, after a $2 million facelift, the Civic Light Opera relocated from the smaller Curran Theater to the twenty-five hundred-seat former movie palace. On rare occasions, when the Warfield was not available and the theater's schedule permitted, some pop concerts took place at the restored Orpheum, running the gamut from Sandra Bernhardt to Jerry Garcia, Tom Waits to King Sunny Ade, Erasure to Pat Metheny.

Warfield Theater

982 Market Street

When Bill Graham announced in 1979 that he was producing Bob Dylan's gospel shows at the recently refurbished Market Street movie palace, the comfortable Kabuki Theater was still operating, so Graham may have simply been chasing away one of his pesky competitors.

Opened in 1922, the theater and nine-story office building was constructed for the phenomenal cost of $3.5 million. Opening night featured a film, *The Fourteenth Love,* along with an appearance by its star, Viola Dana, as well as assorted Hollywood figures, including Clara Kimball Young, Lila Lee, Mary Miles Mintner, Thomas Miegham, Hobart Bosworth, Billie Dove, and others. For many years the Warfield programs mixed vaudeville and silent films. Among the vaudeville stars to trod these boards were Al Jolson and Rin Tin Tin. After the death of vaudeville, stage shows did not return to the theater until the forties, when attractions like Louis Armstrong and an aging Bill "Bojangles" Robinson shared the program with movies that now talked.

For a few years after he brought in the controversial Dylan Christian concerts, Graham used the hall only for his more uptown shows: Liza Minnelli, Shirley MacLaine, Broadway road shows. The Grateful Dead recorded a live album at the Warfield during a remarkable fifteen-night run in 1980. But when the Kabuki shut down for good, Graham was able to strike a marvelously advantageous deal with a brother-sister pair who wanted to open a New York–style disco in San Francisco and had dumped nearly a million dollars into renovating a former printing plant for that purpose (before permit problems squelched the project). Graham convinced the hapless couple to pour a similar amount into remodeling the Warfield, including tearing out the seats on the orchestra floor and replacing them with the kind of tiered table-seating that had been the beauty of the now defunct Kabuki, all the while maintaining the master lease for himself. The disco ran on Saturdays only and, within a year, was out of business, although the improvements its owners paid for remained.

Comedian Andy Kaufman, in his lounge-singer guise as Tony Clifton, opened a weekend of 1981 shows by Rodney Dangerfield and so alienated and antagonized the audience that, by the weekend's end, the producers had erected a rope barrier in front of Kaufman/Clifton to keep him from being injured by objects thrown by the audience.

In an unusual move, a band known by the name of its members, Hagar, Schon, Aaronson, Shrieve, recorded its one and only album live at the Warfield in 1984. Elvis Costello brought his unique "Blood and Chocolate" tour to the room in 1986, where he gave a regular concert the first night, played songs selected from a big spinning wheel the next night, and performed an entirely different concert with a completely different band the third night.

Prince joined his protégés, The Bangles, onstage one night at the Warfield in 1986 and apparently liked it so much that he returned a week later to put on a show with his own band. The next year, the Purple One raced over from a sold-out Oakland Coliseum concert to perform a late show of unrecorded songs at the considerably smaller, three-thousand-seat San Francisco theater.

Guns 'N' Roses gave a special "public rehearsal" in 1991 prior to the band's extensive "Use Your Illusion" tour, Axl Rose reading lyrics from teleprompters. Likewise, Pearl Jam, at the time the biggest band in the world, chose to open the band's "Vs." tour at the Warfield. Neil Young and Booker T. and the MGs also previewed their summer 1993 European tour with surprise shows at the Warfield. At one, comedian Dana Carvey was pulled from the audience to do fifteen minutes of stand-up.

Warfield Theater, a three-and-half-million-dollar vaudeville palace. (photographer unknown)

Dawn Club
20 Annie Street

In the summer of 1940, the Hot Jazz Society arranged several sessions for the recently formed Yerba Buena Jazz Band at the Dawn Club in an alley just behind the Palace Hotel. Led by trumpeter Lu Watters, the band quickly proved popular and within months was holding down a four-night-a-week schedule. In the midst of the swing era, Watters and company were determinedly rudimentary, playing classic New Orleans ensemble jazz: ragtime, cakewalks, and blues. When the band re-formed in January 1946 and returned to the Dawn Club after World War II, the Yerba Buena Jazz Band became the focal point of a full-blown Dixieland jazz resurgence. After New Year's Eve 1946, Watters took the band across the bay to a large club in El Cerrito, previously home to fan dancer Sally Rand, which he renamed Hambone Kelly's. Trombonist Turk Murphy split off in 1949 and trumpeter Bob Scobey left the following year. Both led Dixieland bands around the Bay Area for the rest of their lives. But the phenomenon had reached its height in that short timespan after the war at the Dawn Club, where today a brass plaque commemorates the event.

Palace Hotel
Market and New Montgomery streets

Enrico Caruso ran out of the Palace Hotel, where he was staying after an engagement at nearby Wade's Opera House, the morning of the 1906 earthquake and vowed never to return to San Francisco. He never did, but on Christmas Eve 1910, across the street at Lotta's Fountain in a concert sponsored by the *San Francisco Chronicle,* another Italian opera star of the day, Luisa Tetrazzini, gave a performance for one hundred thousand music lovers. Her performance so moved the head chef of the Palace Hotel that he created a special dish in her honor, turkey Tetrazzini. The hotel was also the site of the first public jukebox. President Warren G. Harding died of food poisoning in the hotel on August 2, 1923. Cards allegedly belonging to the deck he was playing solitaire with when the end came used to turn up every so often in Third Street pawnshops.

Mars Hotel

192 Fourth Street

This seedy Skid Row flophouse, long since a worthy victim of urban renewal, was immortalized for its ironic value in the title of the 1974 Grateful Dead album, *From the Mars Hotel*. The hotel was also only a few blocks from the Automatt where the album was recorded.

Wade's Opera House

Mission and Third streets

Built and opened on January 17, 1876, by a local dentist, Dr. Thomas Wade, Wade's Opera House, as it was called, was said to be the largest such theater in the country, with a stage eighty-five feet deep, more than a hundred feet wide, and a hundred feet high. Enrico Caruso sang here the night before the 1906 earthquake, which destroyed the structure.

The Automatt

898 Folsom Street

This converted warehouse was transformed into a three-room recording studio downstairs by Coast Records and leased to CBS Records, while movie director Francis Ford Coppola took over the upstairs for his American Zoetrope offices. The site also became the command post for Columbia Records's beach-head into the San Francisco music scene in 1972. The company installed its Grammy-winning veteran producer Roy Halee (*Bridge over Troubled Water*) to oversee the studio operation—Paul Simon and Art Garfunkel doing separate solo projects were among the new studio's first clients—and established a hope-less artist and repertoire branch that never signed a single successful act. But Columbia acts like Santana, Sly Stone, Boz Scaggs, and a new, all-instrumental rock band named Journey all recorded in the large Studio A, while the smaller Studios B and C were generally rented to outside clients, like Steve Miller, who cut *Fly Like an Eagle* here.

Columbia folded their tent in 1977 and producer David Rubinson, who had taken over the top floor for his offices and turned Studio C into the town's first fully automated studio, assumed the lease and went into the studio business. In addition to Rubinson's own productions of acts at the studio complex (which he renamed the Automatt) such as Labelle, Santana, and Herbie Hancock, Journey did *Departure* and the Clash made *Give 'Em Enough Rope* here. Captain Beefheart did his 1978 album, *Shiny Beast (Bat Chain Puller)*, here. The Grateful Dead recorded *From the Mars Hotel* and Jane Fonda mixed her first exercise record (with engineer Leslie Ann Jones, one of the city's first female engineers and daughter of bandleader Spike Jones) at the studio. Producer Narada Michael Walden cut Whitney Houston's first number one record, "How Will I Know," at the studio. In 1982, after suffering a heart attack, Rubinson decided the studio business was too much strain and closed the place. The building's owner has since leveled the site for a parking lot.

Mime Troupe Loft
924 Howard Street

The line extended down the block and people waited past midnight to enter the cramped quarters that housed the theatrical guerrilla encampment, the San Francisco Mime Troupe. On November 6, 1965, Mime Troupe business manager Bill Graham, who knew nothing about the scene, threw together a program mixing musicians and poets for a benefit to raise money for the Mime Troupe's legal defense fund. The crowded program included Greenwich Village poets-turned-rockers The Fugs, folk guitarist Sandy Bull, a brand-new rock group, who used the loft as rehearsal space, called the Jefferson Airplane, and another rock band centered around the S.F. Art Institute named Mystery Trend. Members of the improvisational comedy group The Committee and Beat poets Lawrence Ferlinghetti and Allen Ginsberg appeared. Graham stood outside the door, gleefully plucking dollar bills from the fingers of people wanting to get in, stuffing the cash in a green cloth bag that, every so often, had to be hoisted by rope upstairs to be emptied because the crush on the stairway was too much to get through. Graham emerged from the experience a changed man. Within days, he was planning his next benefit concert and, by the end of the year, he left the Mime Troupe to enter the rock concert business on his own.

Rolling Stone Offices
746 Brannan Street and 645 Third Street

In the loft above the printing company Garrett Press on Brannan Street, editor Jann Wenner and his small staff rolled out the first issue of his new rock-and-roll newspaper on November 9, 1967. While the twenty-four-page tabloid boasted correspondents as far-flung as Boston (Jon Landau, later manager of Bruce Springsteen) and London, the focus was decidedly local. The top story on the front page concerned the resignation of a San Francisco Top 40 radio program director, and the big back-cover advertisement touted an upcoming concert by Diana Ross and the Supremes at the Oakland Coliseum (perhaps not coincidentally, promoted by the same Top 40 radio station).

In the beginning of 1970, the prosperous flower of underground journalism moved to spanking new offices on Third Street in the freshly remodeled former home of MJB Coffee, a brick warehouse conveniently located across the street from Jerry and Johnny's, an old-fashioned cocktail lounge that became a haven to former hippie staffers now feeling the deadline pressure of big-time journalism. The elevator didn't play Muzak but rather sound effects that varied depending on the direction of the journey. Drummer Buddy Miles, having taken offense at some perceived slight in the magazine's pages, once stormed the portals of the office in an attempt to deal out some harsh comeuppance to the errant journalist in question. By 1975, Wenner packed up his staff, closed his offices, and moved the enterprise to New York. "San Francisco is a provincial backwater," he sniffed goodbye.

Tin Angel
987 The Embarcadero

Peggy Tolk Watkins was one of those offbeat characters who made San Francisco nightlife so colorful and vibrant in the fifties. She cluttered this converted warehouse with curios and found objects of all description. The musical menu varied between Dixieland jazz and folk; Odetta got her start at the Tin Angel, and the Preservation Hall Jazz Band was a regular attraction. Watkins specialized in the original New Orleans musicians, presenting acts like blues singer Lizzie Miles and the George Lewis band that alternated with the San Francisco models like the Turk Murphy and Bob Scobey bands. After a deal to sell the place to the Weiss brothers (who ran Fantasy Records) fell through in 1958, she moved her operation to Sally Stanford's former Nob Hill bordello, a gaudy, ornate club she called the Fallen Angel, and stayed in business there long enough to launch the career of Johnny Mathis. Transplanted New Orleans jazzman Kid Ory ran the wharfside club for a while, although he cleared out Watkins's antiques and painted the interior an antiseptic white. Watkins, who died in 1973, pursued a career as a painter, exhibiting her work once at the de Young Museum. Ironically, her most lasting contribution to pop culture probably comes from posing as a model, with Fantasy's Max Weiss and a friend, for the cover of the first Lenny Bruce album, *Interviews of Our Time*.

Old Waldorf
444 Battery Street

Jeffrey Pollack, a bail bondsman who grew up in the restaurant business, fell into owning a nightclub and running a bar at the corner of California and Divisadero streets. He found it easy enough to fill the ninety-seat club by booking music; Mike Bloomfield used to play for him frequently. Thus emboldened, Pollack took out a bank loan, remodeled an old Foster's cafeteria in the Golden Gateway, and opened the largest nightclub, with six hundred seats, on the West Coast in October 1976. With his background in the bar and restaurant trade (his father ran a number of the city's top eateries), he knew he could make enough money selling drinks to give the entire door charge to the bands. As a consequence, he was able to persuade many acts that would have otherwise played small concerts to work his nightclub instead. In this way, Pollack single-handedly changed the price structure of nightclub bookings across the country.

What the glass-and-brick rectangular room may have lacked in charm, Pollack compensated for with action. New wave, old rock and roll, heavy metal, soul, and r&b—Pollack paraded every act he could find through the room. Elvis Costello made his U.S. debut there (KSAN broadcast the show live) in 1977. Dire Straits played four sold-out shows on the strength of the band's first hit, "Sultans of Swing." U2 and AC/DC passed through before anybody knew who they were. An unknown Metallica played a "Metal Monday" show at the club. Ry Cooder, with John Hiatt in the band, broadcast an Old Waldorf show live on KSAN that was later issued on a promotional disc by his record company. Huey Lewis and the American Express (before the band changed its name) played its second live appearance here, opening for Van Morrison. They were signed to a record deal the next week.

Gary U.S. Bonds, riding the crest of a small comeback, returned to the stage for an encore, only to have Bruce Springsteen step out of the crowd, strap on a guitar, and play the rest of the set. Glenn Frey and Don Henley of the Eagles, with Linda Ronstadt in tow, showed up one night after playing that afternoon before a sold-out Oakland Coliseum Arena audience, to catch Roy Orbison. When Frey heard "Hotel California" on the club's sound system during an intermission, he asked an aide to see if Pollack was paying for a license (he wasn't). Journey chose a three-night run at the Old Waldorf as the place to introduce vocalist Steve Perry, bringing the insecure, slightly gawky singer out with the band to sing three songs on the encores.

But Pollack rubbed Bill Graham the wrong way. Not only was Pollack booking all the exciting up-and-coming talent passing through town (when the best Graham could offer was an opening slot on a concert) but Pollack's abrasive personal style irritated Graham. Eventually Graham decided his only move was to buy the club from Pollack at a price alleged to be three-quarters of a million dollars. Pollack bought two restaurants from his father with the proceeds. Graham's first foray into the nightclub field lasted three years, when he closed down the Golden Gateway in 1983 and moved further into North Beach to open Wolfgang's in a room he bought from—guess who?—Jeffrey Pollack. The next time Pollack opened a restaurant, one of the chief investors was Bill Graham.

Justin Herman Plaza
Market Street and Embarcadero

U2 lead vocalist Bono scaled the jumbled pile of concrete called the Vallancourt Fountain during the song "Pride (In the Name of Love)" and spray-painted a bit of graffiti high on the sculpture: "Rock and Roll Stops the Traffic." During the impromptu concert, planned a mere twenty-four hours in advance, U2 showed up suddenly at noon Wednesday, November 11, 1987, to play a free "Save the Yuppies" concert, which was captured on film and included in the band's 1989 movie, *Rattle and Hum,* as well as on the album of the same name. In addition to some of the band's typical repertoire, U2, feeling frisky that day, tried out some covers of "Helter Skelter," "All Along the Watchtower," and "People Get Ready." The graffiti stunt provided an ad-lib climax to a sunny lunchtime event that stirred controversy in town for a couple of days. Bono tried to stick up for something he called "graffiti artists' rights" and brought sculptor Armand Vallancourt down from Canada to scribble on the U2 stage set during the group's concerts that weekend at Oakland Coliseum Arena.

Bono of U2 sprays the fountain sculpture at Justin Herman Plaza. (1987, photo by Ken Howard)

3

2

1

4

The Neighbor-hoods

Al Jolson in vaudeville ... Louis Armstrong and
Charlie Parker ... the Jefferson Airplane takes
off ... "A Tribute to Dr. Strange" ... the last
Beatles concert ... *Frampton Comes Alive* ...
the S.F. Blues Festival ... Barry Goldwater and
Evel Knievel ... the Laker Airlines era of British
rock ... the first reading of *Howl* ... Otis
Redding and Jimi Hendrix ... the Band throws
"The Last Waltz" ... Robin Williams launches

1 Holy City Zoo
2 Cow Palace
3 St. Francis Fountain
▼ Winterland

San Francisco Bay

N

Beach
North Point
Bay

1
3
2

Columbus

101

Lombard
Greenwich
Filbert
Union

5
6
4

Van Ness
Franklin
Gough
Octavia
Laguna
Buchanan
Webster
Fillmore
Steiner

Divisadero

Presidio

California

23   22

Clement

Geary Blvd.

Post

13   11   7
12   10
8
9

Third St.

16th Ave.

6th Ave.
5th Ave.

Arguello

Fulton

14

Market

Mission

Hayes
Fell
Oak

15

Haight

Lincoln

Vermont

16th St.
17th St.

21   19

16   19th St.

19th Ave.

Dolores

Valencia

S. Van Ness
Mission

Harrison
Treat

17   20th St.

Connecticut

18

24th St.

20

Portola

280

Sloat

Juniper Serra

Ocean Ave.

101

Third St.

280

Geneva Ave.

25

Carter

24

Rio Verde

The Neighbor-hoods

The Musical History Tour

Longshoremen's Hall

400 North Point

"A Tribute to Dr. Strange" started it all on October 16, 1965, at this giant concrete bunker, the Longshoremen's hiring hall. The Charlatans, fresh from a summer-long residency at Virginia City's Red Dog Saloon, and the Jefferson Airplane, in the band's first engagement outside the Matrix, topped the bill, with a group called the Great Society (featuring vocalist Grace Slick), making its second public appearance, and The Marbles. Several hundred of the willfully deranged, many dosed on LSD, made their way to Longshoremen's Hall that night for the first dance-concert produced by the Family Dog.

Two other dances took place at the hall before the end of the year. The second, starring the Lovin' Spoonful, went well, but the third, featuring the Mothers of Invention, had a few problems. There were some fistfights in the crowd and someone broke one of the plate-glass doors. So the Family Dog moved operations. But in January, Ken Kesey and his madcap cohorts sponsored a two-day free-for-all called the Trips Festival at the union hall. Bill Graham was hired to help run the unmanageable event, at which the Grateful Dead and Big Brother and the Holding Company provided the music.

Since then, concerts at the huge hall have been few and far in between. The Dead returned the following year for a second Trips Festival, this time unassociated with the Kesey crowd, and Wendy O. Williams of The Plasmatics, pounding a Cadillac into submission with a sledgehammer during her act, played the hall in the eighties. Nevertheless, this odd-shaped building, built in 1959 at a cost of $1.4 million, served as one of the crucibles of the San Francisco acid-rock scene.

Palace of Fine Arts Theater

3301 Lyon Street

The last remnant of the 1915 Panama Pacific Exposition, a glittering World's Fair during which Maria Montessori ran the nursery school and Thomas Edison and Henry Ford toured the exhibits, the original Palace of Fine Arts was contructed of plaster and burlap, longevity obviously not a prime consideration of noted architect Bernard Maybeck. A group of San Francisco boosters, led by philanthropist Walter Johnson, raised the funds for the rebuilding of the decayed landmark, which was reopened in 1967.

The one-thousand-seat theater on the premises began presenting lectures and concerts three years later. The 1976 Presidential debate between Jimmy Carter and Gerald Ford was televised from the theater and the S.F. Film Festival has held innumerable tributes and gala premieres at the hall. Concerts ranging from Van Morrison, Rickie Lee Jones, Journey, and the Modern Jazz Quartet have taken place here. The Tubes filmed the band's concert for the 1981 home video, *The Completion Backward Principle*, here, and Todd Rundgren conducted the live recording sessions for his 1991 album *2nd Wind* at the elegant theater.

Great Meadow
Fort Mason, Bay and Laguna streets

At its home in this sylvan setting every September, the San Francisco Blues Festival commands one of the most beautiful vistas of any music fest anywhere. Begun by producer Tom Mazzolini in a ramshackle barn on the University of San Francisco campus one rainy weekend in 1971, the homegrown blues festival has become truly international in scope. Virtually every major name in the field has played here: B.B. King, Buddy Guy, Albert King, Bobby Bland, Otis Rush, Robert Cray, and Albert Collins. In addition, Mazzolini has juggled the booking enough to include country, zydeco, cajun, western swing, and almost every form of American ethnic music.

The Matrix
3138 Fillmore

Now a bar that is rather typical of the Marina neighborhood, the building housed a pizza parlor when singer Marty Balin convinced a friend to buy the lease and convert the room into a nightclub where Balin's new, as-yet unnamed rock band could perform. Balin and his music partner Paul Kantner pounded the nails, painted the walls, and made the place ready for the September 13, 1965, debut of the group called the Jefferson Airplane at the last minute. For the next year, the club served as home base for the band and a central headquarters for the burgeoning local music scene.

By the time the band switched female vocalists, bringing in Grace Slick from the Great Society late the next year, appearances at the Matrix by the rapidly ascending group were growing increasingly rare. But other groups stepped in to fill the gap—the Grateful Dead, Big Brother and the Holding Company, Quicksilver Messenger Service, Sopwith Camel, Country Joe and the Fish, and the Steve Miller Blues Band. From out of town, groups like The Doors, Youngbloods, Charlie Musselwhite and the South Side Sound System, Chambers Brothers, and Electric Flag all worked the club. In December 1968, an unknown Texas guitarist named Johnny Winter played second on the bill to country bluesman Lightnin'

Hopkins. Jam sessions took place frequently, pairing guitarslingers like Elvin Bishop and Albert Collins in freewheeling exchanges.

For a short period of time in late 1968, the Dead made a brief, unsuccessful attempt to get rid of two members, Bob Weir and Pigpen, so that the other members could give some experimental performances as Mickey and the Heartbeats at the Matrix. Santana, It's A Beautiful Day, New Riders of the Purple Sage, and Hot Tuna all played the club before it finally closed in 1972. Co-owner Peter Abrams made tape recordings of virtually every night at the club, and his archives provided the source material for two important live albums by the Great Society *(Conspicuous Only in Its Absence)* and some early Steppenwolf recordings when the group was still known as Sparrow.

Six Gallery
3119 Fillmore Street

"The night of the birth of the San Francisco poetry renaissance," said Jack Kerouac. "6 Poets at 6 Gallery" read the postcard. Kenneth Rexroth hosted the event, with Phillip Lamantia (reading the late John Hoffman), Michael McClure, Gary Snyder, Phil Whalen, and Allen Ginsberg on October 13, 1955. But it was Ginsberg who made history that night, for he chose to read a poem he wrote a couple of weeks earlier, which he perhaps never intended anyone else to read, called *Howl.*

Drinking Gourd
1898 Union Street

At this long-standing Union Street folk spot, Marty Balin spotted Paul Kantner trying his hand at hoot night and took him out to discuss plans he had for a new folk-rock group. The pair became the nucleus for the rock band later known as Jefferson Airplane. Balin knew the Gourd well, since he previously belonged to a folk group called the Town Criers that had formed in the back room. The club sauntered into the seventies under the ownership of singer-songwriter Jeffrey Comanor, who once recorded a little-known album for A&M Records but who financed the purchase of the Gourd with royalties from B-sides tunes he wrote for five million–selling singles by groups like the Fifth Dimension.

Jimbo's Bop City

1690 Post Street

Jimbo Edwards first opened the doors to Jimbo's Bop City at the corner of Post and Buchanan Streets, the heart of the thriving Fillmore district, in November 1950 and the music never stopped until redevelopment steamrollered the block twenty-five years later. Every evening, the back room of Jimbo's Waffleshop transformed itself into Bop City, an after-hours club featuring a brew of the city's percolating jazz scene. The North Beach, Nob Hill, and Tenderloin areas would close and musicians and patrons alike would head to the Fillmore district. One night in 1952, Louis Armstrong, fresh from playing the New Orleans Swing House on Post Street, poked his head into Bop City to catch Charlie Parker on the bandstand—the only known instance of these two jazz giants under the same roof at the same time. Dexter Gordon and Frank Foster once went toe-to-toe on dueling tenors, playing "Peridido" for more than two hours until Jimbo had to pull the plug to get them to stop. Billie Holiday showed up one night, coatless and weeping, having just wrapped up her dead poodle in her floor-length mink coat and cremated both. Underage Clint Eastwood used to sneak in to soak up the atmosphere. Kim Novak and Sammy Davis Jr. dropped by. John Handy played the club when he was a teenager.

Melrose Records

1256 Fillmore Street

Eventually another victim of urban renewal, Melrose Records opened in 1940, after owner Dave Rosenbaum moved his Rhythm Records shop off Sutter and Fillmore. Rosenbaum, whose two brothers worked as newspaper writers in San Francisco, not only ran a record store in the middle of a black ghetto but also managed a record label through the forties that had a big hit with "Open the Door Richard" by Jack McVea. His store unwittingly played midwife to the birth of rock and roll in San Francisco, when, during the fifties, white teens trekked down to his Fillmore-district store to buy the latest rhythm and blues records Sherman Clay didn't carry.

The Primalon
1223 Fillmore Street

In 1954, at this skating rink and sometimes ballroom, fifteen-year-old Jamesetta Hawkins approached bandleader Johnny Otis. Hawkins, who sang as a member of a trio of girls called the Creolettes, had written a song she wanted the rhythm and blues talent scout and record producer to hear. He auditioned the girls at his nearby hotel room and liked what he heard. The next day, they all drove to Los Angeles together to record the song, "Roll with Me Henry," an answer song written in response to the Hank Ballard and the Midnighters hit, "Work with Me Annie." Otis renamed the group the Peaches and their lead vocalist Etta James. The record turned into a bit hit and began the distinguished career of one of the great rhythm and blues vocalists of all time.

Miyako Hotel
1625 Post Street

With its proximity to Winterland one block away and the traditional Eastern tolerance for aberrant behavior, the Miyako became the rock hotel of favor in San Francisco through the seventies. The little Shinto shrines in each room only added to the serene atmosphere of a place that proved it could put up with anything over the time lunatic rockers patronized the Japantown hotel. After "The Last Waltz," cast and crew convened in the Garden Bar downstairs, where Bob Dylan and Dr. John shared the keyboard long into the evening, as Eric Clapton, Muddy Waters, Neil Diamond, and others watched. After the band's final performance down the street, the Sex Pistols returned to the Miyako and broke up for good during an acrimonious meeting in manager Malcolm McLaren's room.

Kabuki Theater
1881 Post Street

The cineplex currently housed in the west end of the Japantown center was built in 1960 as the Kabuki Theater, a $4 million dinner theater that seated nine hundred at tiered tables on the main floor and another five hundred on a small balcony. In 1981, the Bill Graham organization started throwing about sixty shows a year at the hall, a perfect balance of size, sightlines, and acoustics. During the Laker Airlines era of rock, when MTV vaulted a new British-haircut band onto the charts every month, these groups subsequently paraded across the Kabuki stage regularly: the Eurythmics, Dexy's Midnight Runners, ABC, Men at Work, Frankie Goes to Hollywood, Fun Boy Three. Huey Lewis and the News anointed their breakthrough success of *Sports* with a gala run at the Kabuki in 1983. Eddie Money filmed a cable TV special at the club. Metallica made the band's first headline concert anywhere at the Kabuki. It all came to an end in 1984, when the Hawaii-based owners of the property sold the building for $3.5 million.

Fillmore Auditorium
1805 Geary Street

Although producer Bill Graham only operated the small upstairs ballroom from January 1966 to July 1968, in that short time, he managed to make the long-standing Fillmore district dance hall a world-renowned institution, synonymous with the new rock sound of the sixties. Not only did the San Francisco bands of the day—Jefferson Airplane, the Grateful Dead, Big Brother and the Holding Company, Quicksilver Messenger Service, Moby Grape, Santana, Creedence Clearwater Revival—make their first important performances on this stage, but similar groups from all over the world came to play the Fillmore: Cream, Jimi Hendrix, Pink Floyd, Traffic, Led Zeppelin, The Who, and Velvet Underground.

First opened as the Majestic Hall and Majestic Academy of Dancing in 1912, black promoter Charles Sullivan took over the operation in 1952 and presented the typical laundry list of ghetto attractions, from Duke Ellington and Ray Charles to Little Richard and the Temptations. Sullivan booked West Coast tours of James Brown, Ike and Tina Turner, and Bobby Bland, but had backed away from the concert business by the time Graham stumbled across the hall looking for a place to produce the second Mime Troupe benefit in December 1965, a fundraiser for the legal defense of the guerrilla theatrical troupe Graham managed.

Fillmore Auditorium under seismic retrofit. (1992, photo by Dan Dion)

The Musical History Tour

With his famous barrel of free apples invariably greeting customers at the top of the stairs, Graham produced an extraordinary number of historic shows. Grace Slick made her debut with the Jefferson Airplane at the Fillmore, after playing the room a number of times with the Great Society (and even having her picture on one of the famed Fillmore posters). Lenny Bruce gave his final performance at the hall. Cream recorded a live album *(Wheels of Fire)* and guitarist Eric Clapton later declared the Fillmore engagement the high point of the trio's short career. Chuck Berry recorded a live album backed by the Steve Miller Blues Band, *Live at the Fillmore.* Albert King also recorded his classic live album, *Live Wire,* here, as did jazz flautist Charles Lloyd. Graham also delighted in mixing soul, blues, and rock on the same bills. Otis Redding, Count Basie, Muddy Waters, The Staples, Jimmy Reed, Roland Kirk, and Howlin' Wolf were all among the giants of black music to traipse across the stage under a blaze of psychedelic lights.

Briefly after Graham vacated the club in the summer of 1968, the Flamin' Groovies booked some shows, managing a memorable bill combining MC5, the Stooges, and Alice Cooper, which was attended by almost nobody. The hall stayed dark for the next decade. In the early eighties, renamed the Elite Club by the retired postal-workers group that ran the room, punk rock shows with Black Flag, Dead Kennedys, Public Image Ltd., and Flipper brought live music back to the Fillmore. Bert and Regina Kortz bought the hall in the mid-eighties and refurbished the hall. Graham began to dabble in renting the room. He produced salsa bandleader Ruben Blades there and threw a nostalgic twentieth-anniversary party for his company. He shot an HBO special at the hall. In 1988, he began, once again, producing shows regularly at the Fillmore.

In the next year-and-a-half, acts streamed through: the Red Hot Chili Peppers, Carlos Santana and Wayne Shorter, Iggy Pop, Laura Nyro, Midnight Oil, Jimmy Cliff, Little Feat, Leonard Cohen, Jane's Addiction, Buck Owens, The B-52's. A Neville Brothers concert was interrupted when a four-alarm fire burned down the old synagogue next door and the audience was evacuated. In 1989 an earthquake damaged the aged building and the next four-and-a-half years were spent pouring more than a million dollars into the walls and floors before the Graham organization reopened the hall with a gala month of shows in 1994, inaugurated by a special performance by the Smashing Pumpkins. The hall continued to hold sentimental appeal to other people than those in the Graham organization. Eric Clapton returned to the Fillmore for three nights in 1994 to film the television special for his *From the Cradle* blues album.

The Neighborhoods

Winterland

Post and Steiner streets

Although Bill Graham had used this old ice rink before, when the Paul Butterfield Blues Band/Jefferson Airplane double bill in 1966 drew crowds that were too big for the Fillmore, Winterland became his primary realm of operation after he closed the Fillmore West in 1971. Graham filled the relatively intimate fifty-four hundred-seat hall until he moved on in 1978.

Nevertheless, during the Fillmore/Fillmore West years, a number of noteworthy events took place at Winterland. Janis Joplin made her disastrous San Francisco solo debut here after leaving Big Brother and the Holding Company. The Grateful Dead recorded the 1970 so-called "skull and roses" live album at the hall and returned for a five-night "retirement" engagement in 1975, which the band filmed for *The Grateful Dead Movie* and recorded for the live album, *Steal Your Face*. Jimi Hendrix played one of the greatest gigs of his career at the hall in 1968, with John Mayall's Bluesbreakers (with Mick Taylor on guitar) and Albert King on the bill. The Hendrix performance, which included guest bassist Jack Casady of the Jefferson Airplane, was eventually released on CD years after, circulating as a prized bootleg. The Band chose Winterland as the site of the public debut of the group following the 1969 release of *Music from Big Pink*. Guitarist Robbie Robertson was so ill that night that a hypnotist had to be summoned simply to get him onstage.

But as home to concerts virtually every week through the seventies, Winterland hosted some amazing performances from literally hundreds of bands, not the least of which were the four shows in 1972 by the Rolling Stones, given as a kind of gesture of apology to the Bay Area for the band's previous local appearance at Altamont. Steely Dan once opened a show starring Humble Pie and Slade. Aerosmith once opened for Mott the Hoople and Bachman-Turner Overdrive.

Winterland decked out for "The Last Waltz." (1978, photo by Gary Fong)

Of course, Winterland is best known as the site of San Francisco music's finest moment, "The Last Waltz," on Thanksgiving 1976, when The Band returned to the site of its first appearance under that name to play its final performance with guests Eric Clapton, Muddy Waters, Van Morrison, Neil Young, Joni Mitchell, Neil Diamond, Dr. John, Ringo Starr, Ronnie Hawkins, and others, all captured on film by director Martin Scorsese. Peter Frampton recorded his best-selling *Frampton Comes Alive* at the hall over three nights in 1975. The Sex Pistols ended the band's U.S. tour—and its career—with a Winterland show in January 1978. Graham closed Winterland that New Year's Eve with a rollicking show featuring the Grateful Dead and the Blues Brothers.

After the 1906 earthquake destroyed Grauman's Unique Theater on Market Street, a tent was leased from an Oakland evangelist and erected on an empty lot at the site. Work crews built walls and a roof of corrugated tin around the tent and promoters kept up the three-show-a-day schedule. A little known performer named Al Jolson was one of the star attractions at the vaudeville performances. He complained that when it rained, the sound from the roof drowned out his singing. The Graumans built a ramp from the stage into the middle of the audience, the better for Jolson to be heard. In 1928, the New Dreamland Rink, built at a cost of more than $1 million, replaced the old ice rink on the lot and the owners mixed performances by the San Francisco Opera with boxing matches. For years, Winterland, as the hall was renamed in the forties, was home to the Ice Follies. The building was torn down in 1985 to make room for condominiums.

Both/And

620 Divisadero Street

Janis Joplin dropped by this well-known jazz club one night to catch Big Mama Thornton and heard a song she had never heard before: "Ball and Chain." She and the other members of Big Brother and the Holding Company went backstage afterward to ask Big Mama if they could do the song. Big Mama was a Both/And regular, who even appeared on the 1966 benefit for the jazz club at the Fillmore Auditorium that also featured Jon Hendricks, Denny Zeitlin, Elvin Jones, Randy Weston, and Jefferson Airplane.

Opened in April 1965 on the site of Mr. Smith's Stereo Club, the club launched the John Handy Quintet (the saxophonist still lives in the neighborhood). Miles Davis played the club in 1967, but, over the years, the club gravitated toward the more experimental side of the jazz world: Archie Shepp, Pharoah Sanders, Herbie Hancock, Joe Henderson, and Cecil Taylor. The club moved from its original site three blocks away to larger quarters, where the previous owner had been convicted of arson trying to burn the place down.

After the Both/And went out of business in the mid-seventies, it was operated as the VIS Club for a few years, booking a mix of blues and jazz (Etta James used to play there), before Jurg and Brook Spoerry bought the large room and established the Kennel Club, which became headquarters of the city's booming alternative rock scene starting in 1987. The Spoerrys got out of the business seven years later, only to reassume ownership after the new proprietors failed to make their bank note.

Sly Stewart Residence
155 Haight Street

Even though he was already a successful record producer making hit records with Bobby Freeman and the Beau Brummels at Autumn Records and a well-salaried disc jockey delivering his nightly spiel at Oakland soul station KDIA under the name Sly Stone, Stewart stayed close to the street, living in this bustling ghetto neighborhood in 1964. He even had his number listed in the phone book.

Potrero Theater
308 Connecticut Street

Opened in 1914 as the Alta Theater and operated since 1931 as the New Potrero, this run-down old movie hall had been closed for two years when the Grateful Dead made it the band's first rehearsal hall in San Francisco. Mountain Girl remembers refusing to go back inside after she saw rats running around. Empty for years after, the place was finally purchased and the facade and interior renovated in 1992.

McKinley Park
20th and Vermont streets

This little known hilltop patch of a park with its sweeping view of the Mission district contains a swingset that played a prominent role in the popular MTV video of "What's Up" by 4 Non Blondes. Vermont Street heads over the hill, snaking down in a curlicue as crooked as the famed section of Lombard Street, although tourists and most San Franciscans know nothing of this other winding street.

St. Francis Fountain

2801 24th Street

The real Hard Rock Cafe, the St. Francis Fountain is an old-fashioned malt shop straight out of Ricky Nelson's dreams. Opened in 1918 by James Christakes, a native of Sparta, Greece, it is still operated today by his grandson, Jim Christakes, and his cousin, David Milne, who lives upstairs in the apartment where his partner was born. Vic Morobito used to meet with his buddies over lunch in one of the cozy wooden booths and plot the formation of a professional football team, eventually called the San Francisco 49ers, an event commemorated on the menu by the 49er special. Time stops in 1949 at the St. Francis, where they still make all their own candy and ice cream in the back. There is more real rock and roll to this magical place than all the Hard Rocks and Halls of Fame rolled up in one.

St. Francis Fountain and owner Jim Christakes. (1995, photo by Keta Bill Selvin)

415 Records Office

Redstone Building, 2940 16th Street

From a tiny two-room office in the former Labor Temple, Howie Klein conducted his empire during the early eighties. Klein and partner Chris Knab were deejays and new-wave enthusiasts, who decided to release some demo tapes by local punkers, The Nuns. Picking a name for their label that honored both the area code and police radio signal for disturbing the peace, they made a second record, a single by Pearl Harbor and the Explosions that was produced by a second engineer at Wally Heider's studio named David Kahne. Warner Brothers signed the act basically on the strength of regional sales of the 415 Records single.

Kahne, who went on to become the label's unofficial house producer, took another unknown act, Romeo Void, into the studio and drew international acclaim with the band's debut album. Before long, the major labels came courting and Klein signed a distribution deal with monolithic Columbia Records, where he released albums by Wire Train, Red Rockers, Translator, Until December, and Void. While none of his acts ever tore up the best-selling charts in those heady days, Klein himself wound up president of Reprise Records and producer Kahne head of Sony Records's artist and repertoire division, the Grammy-winning producer of the Tony Bennett album, *MTV Unplugged*.

Globe Theater
2731 Mission Street

The long-gone Globe Theater, which disappeared sometime before World War I, was the scene of some of the early triumphs in the career of Al Jolson, who arrived in San Francisco one week after the 1906 earthquake, the city still a smouldering ruin. For the next two years, he played the city's ten-cent vaudeville houses and, at the Globe, not only met his first wife, Henrietta Keller, an aspiring actress appearing on one of the same bills, but began to develop a modest following for the first time in his brief career, giving him the impetus to move to New York and try Broadway.

Deaf Club
530 Valencia Street

One of the stranger scenes on the punk rock scene during the early eighties was ear-shattering, heavy-artillery live performances in this upstairs room, while the club's regular members sat around the perimeter, smiling and speaking to one another in sign language. Some admitted to actually feeling the vibrations, but regardless, these older, decidedly square people were the perfect hosts for the unruly youths who came to slam dance the night away.

Holy City Zoo
408 Clement Street

This little closet of a nightclub under the Last Day Saloon where local rockers have held forth for two decades played a giant role in the San Francisco comedy scene through the seventies and eighties. A folk club that gradually converted to comedy, the Zoo became the first place every comedian to emerge from San Francisco during that era tried his or her stand-up act. The Zoo roll call reads like a Who's Who of S.F. comedy: Robin Williams, Bob Goldthwaite, Dana Carvey, Kevin Nealon, Mike Pritchard, Bobby Slayton, Will Durst, Jim Samuels (one of the Zoo's final owners), and A. Whitney Brown. In 1977, TV producer George Schlatter signed four Zoo regulars for his reprised edition of *Laugh-In*— Robin Williams, Jim Giovanni, Bill Rafferty, and Toad the Mime. On closing night in 1984, comic Perry Kurtz rented a chain saw to carve the stage into souvenirs, which he waved menacingly at Zoo manager John Cantu. "I'd give Cantu's right arm to keep this club open," he said.

Marty Balin Apartment
290 16th Avenue

Living at this apartment in 1965 with his roommate Bill Thompson, who worked at the *San Francisco Chronicle* as a copy boy, Marty Balin used to talk about his idea of an electric folk-rock band that would combine the rock-and-roll sensibilities of the Beatles with the kind of tight-harmony folk music Balin sang with his group, the Town Criers. He had separated from his wife and their young child and was looking for new avenues to explore. He took his first acid trip with Thompson and, while they were walking through Golden Gate Park long after dark, a knife-wielding mugger jumped out of the bushes. "Wow, man," said Balin, "that sure is a beautiful knife." The would-be assailant counseled Thompson to get his obviously demented friend some professional help and retreated into the darkness. A poet, painter, dancer, and Washington High graduate whom Johnny Mathis once complimented for his singing, Balin was also schooled in the printing trades, his father's profession, and was looking for a job as a printer when he ran into Paul Kantner one night that year at the Drinking Gourd. The Jefferson Airplane began to evolve from a dream into a plan.

Cow Palace

Geneva Boulevard, Daly City

Shirley Temple Black visited the Beatles backstage at the Cow Palace, although the cheeky Brits really didn't have any idea who she was. The Beatles came here in August 1964, the opening night on the band's first U.S. tour. The group returned the following year to the seventeen thousand-seat hall, where rock concerts had been held with great regularity since Chubby Checker headlined "Twist Party" in 1962. Disc jockeys Tom Donahue and Bobby Mitchell produced a lineup of a dozen acts, promoted the show via their KYA radio shows, and even formed a record company to release a live recording of one of the shows titled *Memories of the Cow Palace*. The lineup for the 1965 "Fall Spectacular" was typical: Sonny and Cher, The Byrds, Lovin' Spoonful, Little Anthony and the Imperials, Bobby Freeman, Beau Brummels, Glen Campbell, Charlie Rich, the Shangri-Las, and others.

Producer Bill Graham did his first concerts at the Cow Palace while he was still running the Fillmore Auditorium, bringing first Donovan and then The Doors into the much larger venue. Through the seventies and eighties, he brought act after act, including an annual New Year's Eve show, into the historic building: Paul McCartney, the Rolling Stones, Pink Floyd, and Neil Diamond. Elvis Presley played the Cow in 1970. Nirvana headlined a benefit here in 1993.

George Harrison hit the hall on the third stop of his 1973 tour, by which time his voice was already shot, as he croaked his way through "Something" and the rest of his pathetic performance. The Who opened the band's "Quadrophenia" tour

Cow Palace ready for the Republican convention. (1956, photo by Ken McLaughlin)

at the Cow Palace in a show that was never to be forgotten. Drummer Keith Moon passed out not once, but twice. After the second time, guitarist Pete Townshend simply shrugged his shoulders and approached the microphone. "Is there a drummer in the house?" he asked. Some young fan scambled up out of the arena floor and finished the set with the band.

Built as a livestock show grounds, the site of the first Grand National Livestock Exposition was held in November 1939. The arena had gained its unusual name from some sarcastic newspaper writer, who, during the building's construction, sniffed in print, "While people are being evicted from their homes, a palace is being built for cows."

The Republicans held their national convention here in 1956, when Eisenhower was nominated for a second term, and, again, in 1964, when Barry Goldwater was the party's nominee. The Cow Palace has hosted circuses, religious revivals, basketball, ice hockey, tennis, track and field, boxing, professional wrestling, and indoor auto racing, including a two-night run by motorcycle daredevil Evel Knievel in 1970. A wall in the ticket office displays autographs from Cow Palace headliners, beginning with Bob Hope in 1963.

Candlestick Park
off Highway 101, San Francisco

Although there have only been four rock concerts in the history of the stadium that opened with the S.F. Giants' 1960 season and has been home to the 49ers since 1971, the Beatles' final public performance took place out by second base on the chilly, windswept night of August 29, 1966, and the sports park thus earned its lasting place in rock history. A crowd of 25,000 watched the lads roll onto the field in a Loomis truck, bash out eleven songs in thirty minutes and depart with the same dispatch with which they had arrived. In all, the Beatles spent five hours in San Francisco that day.

In addition to the Fab Four swan song, a peculiar fundraiser in the seventies hosted by Top 40 deejay and waterbed salesman Tom Campbell featured The Stories, who had a popular hit at the time with "Brother Louie." The 1981 Rolling Stones tour stopped at Candlestick; so did the 1983 "Monsters of Rock" extravaganza starring Van Halen, the Scorpions, and a little-known band called Metallica. Bill Graham ran a pool backstage that day, betting on exactly how far into his appearance on stage it would be before Van Halen vocalist Sammy Hagar would say "fuck." Estimates ranged from three seconds to five minutes. When Hagar's manager got wind of the pool, he bought everything over five minutes and took the pot. Hagar waited more than eight minutes. A conspiracy? Graham always suspected it.

The Beatles call it quits at Candlestick Park. (1966, photographer unknown)

The Musical History Tour

5

East
Bay

2

1

"W.P.L.J." by the Four Deuces ... LSD by
Owsley ... Steve Miller blues ... Buddy Guy
jams with Cream ... Country Joe and the Fish ...
the trail of the Golliwogs ... *Jimi Plays
Berkeley* ... "Cast Your Fate to the Wind"
to "Proud Mary" ... the Beserkeley Records
guerrillas ... Metallica's garage days ... Benny
Goodman and the birthplace of swing ...
Buck Owens's nightmare nightclub ... Clifton
Chenier's French dances ... Led Zeppelin
under arrest ... the death of Phillipe Wynne ...
the Rolling Stones meet the Hell's Angels ...
Green Day: Pinole to Woodstock

1 Keystone Berkeley
2 Concord Pavilion
▼ Paramount Theater

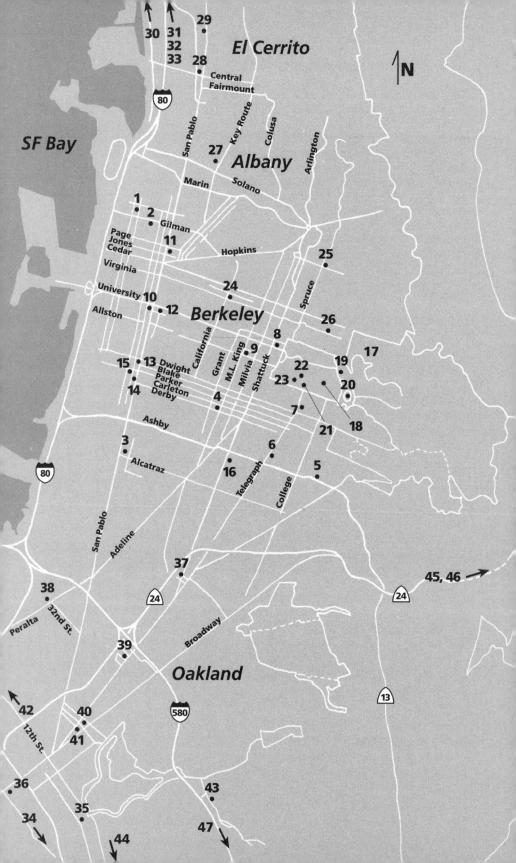

SF Bay

30 31
32 33

29

El Cerrito

N

80

28

Central
Fairmount

San Pablo

Key Route

Colusa

Arlington

27 **Albany**

Marin Solano

1
2
Gilman
11
Page
Jones
Cedar
Virginia

Hopkins

Spruce

25

University 10
Allston 12

24 **Berkeley**

26

8

17

California
Grant
M.L. King
Milvia
Shattuck

9

19
20
22
23

15 13 Dwight
Blake
Parker
Carleton
Derby

7

21 18

14

4

Ashby

3
Alcatraz

6

5

16
Telegraph
College

80

San Pablo
Adeline

37

24

45, 46

38

24

Peralta
32nd St.

Broadway

39

13

Oakland

42

40

580

12th St.

41

36

43

35

34

47

44

East
Bay

1 Cosmo's Factory	**17** UC Berkeley Campus	**35** Henry J. Kaiser
2 Punk Rock Club	**18** Wurster Hall	Auditorium, Oakland
3 Music City Records	**19** Greek Theatre	**36** Ivey's, Oakland
4 Jimi Hendrix's	**20** Memorial Stadium	**37** Omni, Oakland
Boyhood Home	**21** Pauley Ballroom	**38** Duck Kee Market,
5 Ralph J. Gleason	**22** Zellerbach Auditorium	Oakland
Home and Office	**23** Harmon Gymnasium	**39** Showcase, Oakland
6 Country Joe and	**24** The Green Factory	**40** Paramount Theater,
the Fish Apartment/	**25** Home of the Hits	Oakland
Jabberwock	**26** Maybeck Recital Hall	**41** McFadden's Fabulous
7 Larry Blake's	**27** John Fogerty Studio,	Ballroom, Oakland
8 Keystone Berkeley	Albany	**42** Continental Club,
9 Berkeley Community	**28** Metallica House,	Oakland
Theater	El Cerrito	**43** Earl (Fatha) Hines
10 Mandrake's	**29** Arhoolie Records/	Home, Oakland
11 New Orleans House	Down Home Music,	**44** Frenchy's, Hayward
12 Freight & Salvage	El Cerrito	**45** Brent Mydland Gravesite,
13 Longbranch	**30** St. Mark's Catholic	Oakmont Cemetery,
14 Ruthie's Inn	Church, Richmond	Lafayette
15 Fantasy Records	**31** Sam's Club, Richmond	**46** Concord Pavilion,
16 Monkey Inn	**32** The Shire, El Sobrante	Concord
	33 Rod's Hickory Pit, Vallejo	**47** Altamont Speedway,
	34 Oakland Coliseum	Livermore
	Arena and Stadium,	
	Oakland	

The Musical History Tour

Cosmo's Factory
1230 Fifth Street, Berkeley

Creedence Clearwater named the band's sixth and most successful album after these warehouse headquarters in industrial Berkeley. The musicians pulled their cars inside, arriving promptly every weekday around noon. A small loft served as the office and a blue-curtained area in the corner of the floor served as the actual rehearsal hall. The rest of the space was given over to equipment storage and maintenance. It was the group's practice to rehearse the basic tracks to albums at the Factory for as many as six weeks prior to recording. The name for the rehearsal hall came from a gag someone made at the previous headquarters, a small back room in Richmond, where drummer Doug Clifford complained about the working conditions, only to hear "Well, it's better than working in a factory." In his honor, they added his nickname, Cosmo, to the name. The band filmed a noteworthy jam session with Booker T. and the MGs at the Factory for a 1971 television special. After the band dissolved in 1972, drummer Clifford and bassist Stu Cook bought a remote recording van and, for several years, maintained the place, most recently as a warehouse and production facility for the Berkeley Repertory Theater for their own production company, where they worked with the Valley Boys, the Don Harrison Band, Roky Erikson and Doug Sahm, among others.

Creedence Clearwater's sixth album was named after Cosmo's Factory. (1995, photo by David F. Selvin)

Punk Rock Club
924 Gilman Street, Berkeley

A nightclub known only by its address, 924 Gilman Street has been the East Bay home of punk rock since the mid-eighties, when this unique collective first evolved. The only rock spot in the area that admits minors, the place operates as a private club and sells memberships at one counter, tickets at another. It has been a sanctuary for wayward youth and disaffected teens since its opening in the early eighties and was the haven where Green Day got its chops in between grassroots road trips before multiplatinum *Dookie*, Woodstock '94, and MTV. In 1994, Jello Biafra of the Dead Kennedys sustained serious injuries after a beating he received in the mosh pit from some skinhead patrons unimpressed with Biafra's punk credentials.

Music City Records
1866 Alcatraz Street, Berkeley

Owner Ray Dobard used to keep a clock above the counter made out of his one big hit record, "W.P.L.J." by the Four Deuces. An archetypal doo-wop record of the era, the 1955 single later turned up in a cover version by the Mothers of Invention on the album *Burnt Weeny Sandwich* (Frank Zappa even included a remake of the single's B-side, "Here Lies Love," on *You Can't Do that Onstage Anymore, Vol. 5*). Although "W.P.L.J." may have been the best-known record on the label Dobard ran out of the back of the typical ghetto retail record store, he continued to have modest local success right into the seventies, although his only recording to make the national charts always remained the 1956 r&b instrumental, "Johnny's House Party" by Johnny Heartsman.

Jimi Hendrix's Boyhood Home
Martin Luther King Way and Derby Street, Berkeley

The site of Savo Island Village, an early low-rent housing project for Navy families, was long ago given over to the Berkeley public schools and torn down. But infant Jimi Hendrix, at age two still named Johnny Allen Hendrix, abandoned by his mother, was living in Savo Island with a friend of his grandmother when his father returned from the Army, moved him back to Seattle, and changed his name to James Marshall Hendrix.

Ralph J. Gleason Home and Office
2830 Ashby Avenue

The first daily newspaper columnist to cover pop music, Ralph Gleason lived in this comfortable home with his family until he retired from the *San Francisco Chronicle* in 1970 to work for Berkeley's Fantasy Records. Although best known as a jazz reviewer, Gleason roamed far and wide for his writing, from interviewing Hank Williams to reviewing early rock-and-roll shows by Fats Domino and Elvis Presley. His conversion to the cult of Dylan and subsequent support of the early San Francisco rock scene gave the music important critical credibility nationwide. From his office in this house, he not only composed his columns for the paper (which he delivered via the transbay bus that stopped outside), he became a contributing editor (and investor) in *Rolling Stone* magazine from the first issue on.

Ralph J. Gleason's home and office. (1995, photo by David F. Selvin)

Country Joe and the Fish Apartment, Above the Jabberwock
2901 Telegraph Avenue, Berkeley

In the apartment building above this stalwart Berkeley folk club where guitarist Robbie Basho also lived, Joe McDonald, Barry Melton, and Bruce Barthol evolved from a folkie jug group with a political bent to the eclectic acid-rock band that eventually held down centerstage at Woodstock. The trio ambled down to the Cabale, a folk club on San Pablo Avenue, one night in 1965 to try out McDonald's new composition, "Bass Strings," an ode to pot smoking, using amplified equipment. They then knew that for them some undefined line had been breached.

The Jabberwock, less than a mile down Telegraph Avenue from the UC Berkeley campus, was one of the main folk and blues outlets in Berkeley. When rock swept through the folk circles, the club made tentative adjustments. Country Joe and the Fish practically served as house band from 1965 through 1966 and the Cleanliness and Godliness Skiffle Band also played the room frequently. The club did not survive into the seventies.

Larry Blake's
2367 Telegraph Avenue, Berkeley

A fixture on Telegraph Avenue since 1939, Larry Blake's has fed generations of underclassmen their steak and potatoes. Downstairs, the Rathskellar, with its sawdust-covered floor, has been the longest-standing beer bar adjacent to the UC Berkeley campus. Glossy photos on the staircase attest to the veterans of the blues circuit who have played the basement room. During the late seventies, guitarist Tim Kaihatsu, a veteran of Charlie Musselwhite's bands, put together a house band to back up visiting performers, which came to be called the Rat Band. A young bluesman out of Portland, Oregon, named Robert Cray used to stop by and jam when he was in town. Once Cray broke the one million-selling barrier with his album, *Strong Persuader,* he went back to the Rathskellar and, one by one, cherrypicked the members of the Rat Band until every one eventually belonged to his touring band.

Keystone Berkeley
2119 University Avenue, Berkeley

Creedence Clearwater Revival played the band's first gig under its new name at a beer bar on this site called the New Monk, a former grocery store. The group even performed on a flatbed truck, while club management handed out free beer, at a noontime concert next to Sproul Plaza to help promote the club. New Monk quickly became a hangout for the beleaguered frat crowd, an endangered species in those long-haired days. When Freddie Herrera of Keystone Korner took over in 1972 and called it Keystone Berkeley, the room started the longest successful run of any rock club in town. For the next twelve years, the six hundred-capacity club was the prime spot for rock in Berkeley, hosting Van Morrison, John Lee Hooker, the Doobie Brothers, Boz Scaggs, Tower of Power, Earth Quake, Stoneground, Mike Bloomfield, Albert King, Herbie Hancock, and the Pointer Sisters.

Berkeley Community Theater

Milvia Street and Allston Way

As his days at the Fillmore West were ending in the early seventies, Bill Graham discovered that for a nominal fee he could reserve open dates at this auditorium and tie up the building from any potential competitor. He began to book reserved-seat shows into this thirty-three hundred-seat auditorium on the Berkeley High School campus with greater regularity. Before Graham started using the hall, the Berkeley Community Theater was the site of occasional concerts and road-show musicals. Bob Dylan played an acoustic concert there in February 1964 and again in December 1965 with Canadian rock-and-rollers The Hawks backing him up. The Byrds played an after-school concert there for students in 1965. The film *Jimi Plays Berkeley* comes from a Memorial Day 1970 performance at the hall. Sixteen-year-old Neal Schon sat in with Derek and the Dominos at the group's Bay Area concert here the following year and guitarist Eric Clapton invited the prodigy to join the band permanently (he opted to join Santana instead). The Who put on a devastating performance at the hall the same year, a show Pete Townshend still remembered as one of the two or three best the band ever gave when he returned to the Berkeley Community for a solo show in 1992.

Mandrake's

1048 University Avenue, Berkeley

An old pool hall reopened as a beer bar and nightclub in 1969 by an ex-schoolteacher and blues fan named Mary Moore, Mandrake's had Muddy Waters and Charlie Musselwhite as the club's opening acts. It was home away from home for Chicago bluesmen like Waters, John Lee Hooker, and Magic Sam, even if it was Berkeley-based rock bands like the Loading Zone, Commander Cody and His Lost Planet Airmen, and Joy of Cooking who payed the bills at the club during its brief reign.

New Orleans House

1505 San Pablo Avenue, Berkeley

Eric Clapton and Jack Bruce finished playing the Fillmore with their band Cream and dashed across the Bay Bridge to catch the late set by Chicago blues guitar whiz Buddy Guy. They couldn't resist getting onstage and jamming. These kinds of impromptu collaborations were part of the loose, intimate atmosphere of this homey Berkeley club with its hot apple cider. Guitarist Guy, in fact, recorded his 1968 Vanguard album, *This Is Buddy Guy,* at the two hundred-seat club. The acoustic duo of Jorma Kaukonen and Jack Casady that was called Hot Tuna cut its first album live at the New Orleans House. Jazz-rock group Fourth Way also did a live album at the club.

Opened in 1967 by Kitty Griffin, who taught handicapped children by day and ran the club at night, the New Orleans House presented the gamut of the local rock scene in its day, including Sons of Champlin, Boz Scaggs, Tower of Power, and SeaTrain. It also operated briefly in the seventies under the name West Dakota, a club whose owners included music-business attorney Dick Hodge, who was later elevated to the judicial bench in Alameda County.

Freight & Salvage
1111 Addison Street

Although the renowned folk club only caught the tail end of the folk renaissance when it opened in 1968, the site has managed to outlast more famed stops on the troubadour trail across the country. Originally located two blocks north of its current site on San Pablo Avenue, the club took its name from the building's previous tenant, a used-furniture store. Mixing a program of folk-festival regulars like Dave Van Ronk, Mance Lipscomb, the Reverend Gary Davis, and Bukka White with local protégés such as Alice Stuart, John Shine, Mary McCaslin, Jody Stecher, and Laurie Lewis, the club soon became central headquarters of the East Bay folk-scene. Terry Garthwaite and Toni Brown of Joy of Cooking, having worked the club with their rock band, chose the Freight as the place to unveil their duo act. In 1983, the club re-formed as a non-profit corporation called the Berkeley Traditional Music Society, and, in 1988, moved to the much larger quarters the Freight now occupies, all the while continuing the five- and six-night-a-week program and an eagle-eyed booking policy that has brought folk-scene newcomers like Michelle Shocked, Christine Lavin, and Greg Brown to the area.

Freight and Salvage: the Bay Area's longest-standing folk headquarters. (1987, photo by Brant Ward)

Longbranch
2505 San Pablo Avenue

Once the site of the folk clubs Babylon and the Cabale, the Longbranch was, in many ways, the archetypal rock club of the seventies. A rough and rude beer bar where drug dealers in Frye boots mingled with grizzled Berkeley hippies, the 'Branch featured a steady assortment of local bands who were stars on Saturday nights at the corner of San Pablo and Dwight Way. Western swing specialists Asleep at the Wheel started at the club in 1972, holding down the stage every Tuesday for many months and drawing a Berkeley countrybilly audience that had been cultivated by Commander Cody and His Lost Planet Airmen.

Earth Quake, Berkeley's Rolling Stones, couldn't get arrested across the Bay despite putting out a half dozen albums and serving as founding act on the pioneering Beserkeley Records label. But the band routinely drew overflow crowds to the seedy dive. Eddie Money, who made the Top 10 with two tracks from his debut album, started out at the 'Branch. His first band, the Rockets, broke up in a fistfight onstage, and later a San Francisco State film student captured Money's aspirations and the Longbranch atmosphere in a film eventually released as *Money Madness*.

The Shakers, who packed the club every Sunday for the better part of a year, were a band of disaffected rockers swept up in the Berkeley music scene's fascination with Jamaican reggae in the early seventies, although the group's sole album, *Yankee Reggae*, was barely noticed. The Longbranch, in fact, catered to the reggae mood of the town by importing Jamaican talent directly for engagements. Toots and the Maytals, Third World, Soul Syndicate, Eric Donaldson, Dennis Brown and others all appeared at the club during its reggae period.

Ruthie's Inn
2618 San Pablo Avenue

This Quonset hut served as soul central in Berkeley through the seventies. Bobby "Blue" Bland filled the place every time he came through town. Rufus played the band's first Bay Area date at the six hundred-seat club and left angry after failing to draw any customers. The club boasted a counter serving delectable ribs and chicken, Lips 'N Fingers BBQ, in one corner, plus frequent performances by local bluesman L.C. Good Rockin' Robinson, who played tablestand steel guitar, and whose drummer, Teddy (The Chicago Kid) Winston, once, in a moment of inspiration, threw his sticks into the audience, swiveled his chair around, and pounded his fists on the wall behind him.

Fantasy Records
Tenth and Parker streets

After selling some hundred million dollars worth of records with Creedence Clearwater Revival, this onetime jazz specialty label (Vince Guaraldi's "Cast Your Fate to the Wind" was Fantasy's previous biggest hit) built a beautiful new building on this lot and moved its operations out of its overflowing Oakland warehouse in 1970. After the film *One Flew Over the Cuckoo's Nest* won eight Oscars and earned the company even more millions, film producer/label owner Saul Zaentz built a second, larger building next door.

The complex houses some of the finest post-production film facilities in Northern California and the best recording studios in the Bay Area. At first, the studios were built exclusively for Fantasy acts, but in 1980, the company opened the doors to the public. While the label continues to operate out of the building, the facilities get constant use from outside projects. Journey recorded the multi-platinum *Escape* in the giant Studio D. Green Day recorded *Dookie* in the big room. Chris Isaak, Huey Lewis and the News, Eddie Money, Frankie Beverly, Todd Rundgren, Sheila E., En Vogue, among many others, have all recorded hit records in the studios.

Fantasy itself remains one of the country's largest independent labels, although it concentrates on reissuing vintage recordings from the company's vast backlog from both the Fantasy archives and acquired labels like Prestige, Riverside, Milestone, Stax/Volt, Specialty, and Pablo.

Monkey Inn
3109 Shattuck Avenue

Guitarist John Fogerty and drummer Doug Clifford played in a house band with a pair of Cal students at this quintessentially sixties frat hangout, a beer bar and pizza parlor. When the two students graduated in 1964, Fogerty and Clifford brought their regular musical associates in and the Golliwogs became a frequent attraction here, giving the El Cerrito–based band its first taste of local celebrity and earning the group a lot of work at fraternity parties.

Wurster Hall

UC Berkeley campus

Steve Miller arrived in San Francisco and spent his last five dollars to catch his old Chicago buddy Paul Butterfield playing the Fillmore. He climbed onstage to jam and drew an ovation by announcing he was moving to town. He was living in his Volkswagen van, parked on the streets of Berkeley. He summoned his Madison, Wisconsin, colleagues, Curley Cooke and Tim Davis, and located bassist Lonnie Turner, who he met while jamming at the Jabberwock on a scouting trip the previous year. Over the Thanksgiving holiday 1966, Miller convened rehearsals for his new band in the unlocked basement of the architecture department in Wurster Hall. "Jimmy Reed, key of A," Miller told bassist Turner. "Don't do the California turnaround. If you can lock down with the kick and stay in A, we'll get along." The Steve Miller Blues Band made its first public appearance the following week at The Forum, a popular Telegraph Avenue coffeehouse, and, miraculously, were booked to play a date at the Avalon Ballroom in December for the princely sum of $500. Miller rented an apartment and took his band out to dinner and a movie.

Greek Theatre

Gayley Road, UC Berkeley campus

In the only public bequest he made during his lifetime, publisher William Randolph Hearst built this grand marble and concrete amphitheater in memory of his mother, Phoebe Apperson Hearst, the great benefactor of the university who once lived in a home on the campus. Over the years, the Greek Theatre has played host to many official university events, from Charter Day addresses by the distinguished likes of Adlai Stevenson to giant football rallies, complete with mammoth bonfires in the sandy pit in front of the stage. The concrete-lined bowl was the annual location for the Jubilee Concert of the Berkeley Folk Festival, an event that began in the fifties and continued through the next decade, featuring the finest talents in the field. Occasionally, the amphitheater was rented to outside promoters for concerts by the Lovin' Spoonful and comedian Dick Gregory (with Jefferson Airplane as his opening act). Sometimes ambitious student promoters used the site for large-scale productions, such as the three sold-out shows by Boz Scaggs, produced by Cal student Gregg Perloff, who ended up president of Bill Graham Presents. University officials, succumbing to neighborhood pressure, eventually limited the use of the venue for outside music concerts, but the Graham organization has thrown at least a dozen concerts a year at the nine thousand-capacity facility, dug into the hill and often chilled by fog at night but with a spectacular view of the Bay from the upper reaches of the grassy hill at the top.

Many of the biggest names in music have appeared at the Greek Theatre. The Talking Heads put on an absolutely incendiary 1983 concert, a week before filming the concert documentary, *Stop Making Sense,* in Los Angeles. The Grateful Dead put on some memorable shows at the site, including a twenty-year anniversary celebration. The Doobie Brothers recorded the band's 1983 *Farewell Tour* album at the Greek, where the band was briefly joined by original lead vocalist Tom Johnston in a sentimental reunion. Michael Bolton opened for Kenny G., and Elvis Costello gave one of his finest local performances. Pete Seeger and Arlo Guthrie played on one fabulous sunny afternoon, a year after they came through the Greek with Holly Near and Ronnie Gilbert of the Weavers on the HARP tour (the live album of that event may have been recorded in Los Angeles, but the cover photo comes from the Greek). The Bread and Roses Festival presented some extraordinary all-acoustic lineups during the few years producer Mimi Farina mounted the fundraiser, starting in 1977. Fantasy Records released a pair of double-record sets recorded at those signal affairs.

Memorial Stadium

Gayley Road, UC Berkeley campus

When no other appropriate site could be found, the creaky old football stadium that has served the Cal Bears for more than half a century was used for the 1990 Bay Area appearances by Paul McCartney. A widely circulated underground tape, reputedly recorded surreptitiously by one of the sound engineers who isolated the dreadfully off-key background vocals of Linda McCartney, was apparently recorded during those two shows.

Pauley Ballroom

Student Union Building, Sproul Plaza, UC Berkeley campus

Jefferson Airplane and Country Joe and the Fish played a special dance-concert as part of the 1965 Berkeley Folk Festival in this small, utilitarian assembly hall. The Grateful Dead also joined the Fish for a double bill at the hall in December 1966.

Zellerbach Auditorium
Lower Sproul Plaza, UC Berkeley campus

This relatively small theater, seating just under three thousand, has been the location for some memorable music events, such as the Bay Area debut of Nigerian pop star King Sunny Ade or the first local show by the Police. Free concerts outside in Lower Sproul Plaza have been a Cal rock tradition, with bands from Talking Heads to Green Day doing their part.

Harmon Gymnasium
UC Berkeley campus

Rarely used for music events, Harmon Gym was the site for a historic 1966 concert by the Paul Butterfield Blues Band and Jefferson Airplane, which was bassist Jack Casady's first public performance with the band and the group's first major concert appearance outside San Francisco.

The Green Factory
1647 Virginia Street

On February 21, 1965, state narcotics agents raided this home owned by Augustus Owsley Stanley and charged the wayward genius with operating a methedrine factory. Since the raid failed to turn up any of the drug, the state could not get the charges to stick and the court turned the underground chemist loose. Cheeky Stanley even sued the state for the return of his laboratory equipment and won. But, at that stage of the game, even narcs knew little of the mysterious drug LSD and, consequently, missed the opportunity of nipping in the bud the future of the most legendary of all acid manufacturers of the sixties. Stanley's career began unassumingly enough in this modest Berkeley bungalow.

Home of the Hits
1199 Spruce Street

Self-styled "reigning looney" Matthew King Kaufman always compared his Beserkeley Records operation to a guerrilla encampment, and this brown-shingled Berkeley-hills home served as the base of operations. In 1976, despairing of getting another major label record deal for the band he managed, Earth Quake, Kaufman pressed a few hundred copies of the group's new single and got local radio stations to play the record. Before long, he had four different acts in the stable—Earth Quake, Greg Kihn, Jonathan Richman, and The Rubinoos—and European record companies were funding his enterprise. Jonathan Richman scored two consecutive Top 10 hits in England and, Playboy Records, of all labels, was paying to release the records Stateside. Before folding the homegrown label in the early eighties, Kaufman's Beserkeley Records, with its originally ironic slogan "Home of the Hits," scored genuine national success with the Rubinoos and Greg Kihn, whose 1983 single, "Jeopardy," reached all the way to number two.

Maybeck Recital Hall
1537 Euclid Avenue

Originally built by famed architect Bernard Maybeck in 1914 for a popular Berkeley-hills music teacher, this fifty-seat recital hall has become the home of an internationally recognized series of live recordings, *Live at Maybeck Hall.* Among the great jazz pianists participating in the Concord Jazz–produced recordings have been Cedar Walton, Ellis Larkins, Denny Zeitlin, Hank Jones, Sir Roland Hanna, Jaki Byard, Roger Kellaway, Marian McPartland, and Toshiko Akiyoshi.

Pianist Dick Whittington discovered the place, which had been empty for several years, for sale in 1986 and took over the hall and adjacent small apartment. He invited Carl Jefferson of Concord Jazz to record the first recital he presented, by pianist JoAnne Brackeen, and the extraordinary acoustics of the room launched an ongoing program that, so far, has produced more than three dozen acclaimed albums.

John Fogerty Studio
842 Key Route Boulevard, Albany

When John Fogerty, the former Creedence Clearwater mastermind, split Fantasy Records in 1974 in the middle of recording a never-released follow-up to his country and western album, *Blue Ridge Rangers,* he began a long, torturous period of seclusion. He released his first album under his own name the following year, but could never complete a second. Every day, he came and recorded in the studio he built in this flatland residence, a plain, ordinary house he turned into an office and recording studio. He would return the following day and erase the work and start over, a process he repeated for years. After almost nine years of silence, he finally returned with a smash hit, "The Old Man Down the

Road," and a number-one album, *Centerfield*. Although the finished product was recorded at The Plant in Sausalito, every song on the album was blueprinted in this unassuming converted garage on this quiet side street.

Metallica House
3140 Carlson Boulevard, El Cerrito

This shabby, unremarkable house should be a major landmark in the annals of heavy metal rock. Metallica, whose members lived together in the house for three years starting in 1983, wrote, rehearsed, and prepared to record both *Ride the Lightning* and *Master of Puppets* albums in the garage. During this wilderness period, after the release of the ground-breaking *Kill 'Em All* debut, the band spent endless months on the road after the addition to the lineup of guitarist Kirk Hammett, who had moved from San Francisco to nearby El Sobrante during high school (he attended DeAnza High down San Pablo Avenue in Richmond). By the time the band's major-label debut, *Master of Puppets,* started selling serious amounts of records and the band became an authentic attraction on the road, able to headline halls like San Francisco's Kabuki Theater, the small El Cerrito house had served its purpose. But black marks on the garage door still bear witness to the band's spray-painting equipment cases that were once placed in the driveway.

Metallica House. (1995, photo by David F. Selvin)

Arhoolie Records/Down Home Music
10341 San Pablo Avenue, El Cerrito

Chris Strachwitz, a public-school German teacher, Polish immigrant, and die-hard blues fan, spent his summer vacation in 1960 combing Texas with a tape recorder. On the trip, he discovered a sixty-nine-year-old sharecropper in Navasota, Texas, named Mance Lipscomb. The resulting album that Strachwitz released on his own Arhoolie Records became one of the cornerstones of the emerging folk-blues renaissance. Strachwitz himself built one of the most extraordinary bodies of folk and blues recordings in history on his tiny label, including those of Lightnin' Hopkins, Clifton Chenier, Bukka White, and Mississippi Fred McDowell. After recording Country Joe and the Fish as a favor, he wound up owning the publishing rights to "Feel Like I'm Fixin' to Die Rag," which landed no fewer than three million-selling albums for the band. The royalties, combined with the sum earned when the Rolling Stones cut Fred McDowell's "You Gotta Move," allowed Strachwitz to quit teaching and work on his ethnomusicology full-time.

He bought the El Cerrito headquarters for his label in the seventies and established a retail record store, one of the finest outlets for folk, blues, and world music in the Bay Area. Filmmaker Les Blank, who made films with Strachwitz on musicians Lipscomb, Hopkins, Chenier, and others, housed his operation in the back room for several years, and Strachwitz also built an earthquake-proof vault for his tapes and massive collection of 78 r.p.m. records.

St. Mark's Catholic Church
159 Harbor Way, Richmond

A long way from Louisiana, zydeco accordion king Clifton Chenier cut a powerhouse live album in the church gym in 1971 for Arhoolie Records, reissued on compact disc in 1989 as *Live at St. Mark's*. It was Chenier's custom during the seventies to visit the Bay Area, play one or two of the local rock clubs, and participate in a full zydeco fest among the French Louisiannes living in the East Bay who made St. Mark's something of a community center. Chenier would play for five hours, while pots of gumbo steamed on the hot plates in the rear and dancers crowded the gym floor.

Sam's Club

425 Cushing Boulevard, Richmond

This short-lived country and western dive apparently left a lasting impression on young Buck Owens. Although the honky-tonk closed in 1963, Owens wrote a number-one country and western hit in 1967 inspired by this hole-in-the-wall, "Sam's Place." "We played there twice," Owens recalled, "and some guy shot his gun off through the ceiling. And the next time we played there, somebody tried to drive their car through the front door."

The Shire

Tri Lane Road, El Sobrante

The pink house on the crook of this short sidestep off San Pablo Dam Road was decorated with elf runes on the mailbox and called "The Shire" in honor of *The Hobbit*. In 1965, Stu Cook and Doug Clifford lived in what was, at the time, a remote, woodsy location. One night, they and the two other members of their band huddled over the kitchen table, going through three pages of possible new names for the group, finally combining two suggestions to come up with Creedence Clearwater Revival. The band posed for the photos of the cover of their first album among the trees in the backyard.

Rod's Hickory Pit

199 Lincoln Road West, Vallejo

Because the members were in the eighth grade in 1985, their parents had to drive them to the gig, but this long-standing roadside landmark served for the first performance ever by the band that became Green Day. The members grew up across the Carquinez Straits in the lower middle-class town of Pinole.

Oakland Coliseum
Arena and Stadium Complex

695 Hegenberger Road, Oakland

Hot off their latest number-one record, *Soul and Inspiration,* the Righteous Brothers were the first concert attraction at the newly opened Oakland Coliseum Arena in November 1966, but Genesis still holds the arena box-office record with six sellouts. Almost immediately the $25 million modern facility became home to big-time music events, sharing the space with major-league sports teams like the Oakland Raiders, the Oakland A's, and the Golden State Warriors.

Elvis Presley introduced the members of Creedence Clearwater Revival to the audience during his 1970 concert before he sang "Proud Mary." Creedence itself filmed a television concert special at the hall earlier that year. More than twenty years later, Tom Petty and the Heartbreakers filmed their television special here. Over the years, the biggest names in the business have sung in the cavernous basketball arena, from Prince to Kenny Rogers, Diana Ross to the Grateful Dead, John Denver to Blind Faith. Bill Graham first used the Coliseum complex to present the Rolling Stones in 1969, when he got into an onstage fistfight with Stones tour manager Sam Cutler during the band's show.

In 1973, after a couple of experimental forays into outdoor concerts at Kezar Stadium, Graham came to the outdoor stadium with a bill featuring Leon Russell, Loggins and Messina, and Elvin Bishop that he dubbed "A Day on the Green." Inaugurating a Bay Area institution of the seventies, Graham returned to the ballpark the next summer with a concert featuring Crosby, Stills, Nash

Oakland Coliseum Arena lit up at night. (1969, photographer unknown)

and Young and The Band and a second concert starring the Grateful Dead and the Beach Boys. In 1975, he built a castle and drawbridges around the stage and presented "The British Are Coming," a concept concert that packaged Robin Trower, Peter Frampton, Dave Mason, Fleetwood Mac, and Gary Wright. Stadium double bills that summer also included Edgar and Johnny Winter in one show and the Doobie Brothers and The Eagles in another.

Peter Frampton presided over his coronation the following summer in the wake of *Frampton Comes Alive* at a pair of concerts with Fleetwood Mac as the supporting act. Brian Wilson joined his Beach Boys onstage for a couple of songs, the first time in more than twelve years that he appeared with the group he founded, and The Who and the Grateful Dead played a pair of notable concerts in October 1976. The next summer, Fleetwood Mac had broken big enough to headline a concert on their own, and Frampton returned for another pair of sold-out concerts. The Eagles and Steve Miller were also a big show that season, although the grand attraction that summer was the two-day stand by Led Zeppelin that turned out to be the band's final U.S. performance. The Zep weekend was highlighted by an untoward backstage incident involving a Zep security guard and a Graham employee that ended up with Graham and company pressing both criminal and civil charges against the group (only, however, after Zep finished playing the sold-out concerts).

The 1978 season featured shows with the Rolling Stones (on Mick Jagger's birthday), Aerosmith, the Beach Boys, and Linda Ronstadt, and a show featuring Ted Nugent, Blue Oyster Cult, and newcomers Journey. Aerosmith, Nugent, and Journey all returned the following year and Boston opened the summer, but the era was over. As the eighties dawned, only acts that could draw the crowds played the baseball park—Journey, Sammy Hagar and, for a hot moment, REO Speedwagon—but such attractions were getting fewer and farther between.

With *Escape* vaulting the band to the top of the rock pile, Journey brought a visually stunning production to the ballpark in 1983, followed by the reunited Simon and Garfunkel, the Police, and David Bowie, whose ballyhooed "Serious Moonlight" tour fell far short of capacity sales. The following year, on his "Born in the U.S.A." tour, Bruce Springsteen showed enough box-office muscle to sell out two midweek shows. Teen sensations Wham! filled the ballpark that year, as did a heavy-metal rock show featuring the Scorpions, Ratt, Y&T, and young Metallica. But it was clear the era of the ballpark concert had passed, to be reserved for special acts only: the Rolling Stones, Pink Floyd, U2, Bob Dylan backed by the Grateful Dead, and the final tour by The Who.

Henry J. Kaiser Auditorium
10 Tenth Street, Oakland

Old enough to have hosted Buffalo Bill's Wild West Show, the Oakland Auditorium, originally built in 1913, was the subject of a $15 million facelift in 1982 and renamed two years later when it reopened. President Woodrow Wilson spoke here. Jack Dempsey boxed here. It was the longtime home of roller derby's Bay Bombers and the site of the historic 1956 concert by Elvis Presley. The Grateful Dead put on some extraordinary shows at the boomy hall, including a number of New Year's Eve extravaganzas, such as the one when Etta James and the Tower of Power horns joined the band for "In the Midnight Hour" at the appropriate moment. Sergei Rachmaninoff and the Duke Ellington Orchestra played here. Al Jolson, Charlie Chaplin, John Philip Sousa, Isadora Duncan, and Van Halen all appeared at the lakeside auditorium. In 1969, on a seventy-two-hour furlough from serving a life sentence for murdering his wife, country music star Spade Cooley played his last date at the hall, a benefit for the sheriff's association, and died backstage afterward of a heart attack.

Henry J. Kaiser Auditorium. (1995, photo by David F. Selvin)

Ivey's
380 Embarcadero West, Oakland

This Jack London Square club gave soul music a home in downtown Oakland during the eighties and was the scene of one of the genre's more bizarre episodes on July 13, 1984. Phillipe Wynne, ex-lead vocalist of the Spinners on the comeback trail, returned for his encore and was jumping off the stage into the audience when he suffered a fatal heart attack. The audience, thinking it was part of the act, gave him a standing ovation.

Omni

4799 Shattuck Avenue, Oakland

Originally an Italian-American social hall built in 1932, the building was converted to a rather magnificent nightclub in 1985 by millionaire inventor John Nady, whose wireless electric guitar made him a fortune. A frustrated heavy-metal rocker himself, Nady entered the club business, in part so there would be a spot in the area that would book his band, the Nady Alliance. Before he bailed out seven years later, after losing hundreds of thousands of dollars, Nady had expanded his fiefdom to three clubs in three cities, The Stone in San Francisco and One Step Beyond in San Jose. Although his booking policy reflected his interest in ear-shattering teen rock, Nady's Omni did land the occasional news-worthy act, such as the Ice-T gig that took place right at the height of the "Cop Killer" controversy. The club was also the site of the live recording of the 1988 album by Neil Young and the Bluenotes, *This Note's for You.*

Duck Kee Market

3218 Peralta, Oakland

This typical corner store was around the block from the original offices of Fantasy Records in Oakland. When members of Creedence Clearwater took to the street to shoot the cover photo for the band's fourth album, *Willy and the Poor Boys*, the store ended up on the cover of the 1970 million-selling album illustrating the lead-off song, "Down on the Corner."

Showcase

3228 Telegraph Avenue, Oakland

Along with his other Oakland hotspot, the Sportsman's Club, former UC Berkeley All-American Don Barksdale ran the black community's top two nightclubs through the sixties. Everybody on the black-music circuit passed through Barksdale's rooms: B.B. King, Ike and Tina Turner, The Temptations, and Jackie Wilson. His Telegraph Avenue club was a small, long room, with tables closely packed and the back row still very close to the stage, an intimate setting that produced some extraordinary exchanges between musicians and audience. After the shows, the entertainers often repaired to nearby Hi's Restaurant, a twenty-four-hour coffee shop on the corner of Telegraph and MacArthur Boulevard. When Ike and Tina and all the Ikettes piled into the shop, mingling with the neighborhood hookers, it was difficult to tell who was who.

Paramount Theater

2025 Broadway, Oakland

Opened in 1931 on the cusp of the Great Depression, the Paramount Theater was one of the last grand movie palaces built in America. Architect Timothy Pflueger, better known for edifices such as the 450 Sutter Street medical building in San Francisco, lavished on the $3 million theater all the imaginative and extravagant strains of Art Deco he could manage. But, by 1971, the theater was sadly deteriorated from daily use and abuse and closed. In 1973, the luxurious structure returned to life after a full and authentic restoration, scrupulous down to the last detail, as the new home of the Oakland Symphony. In 1977, the Paramount was added to the register of National Historic Landmarks. Because of the heavy schedule demands of the Oakland Symphony and the Oakland Ballet, the Paramount does not rely on outside bookings to fill its schedule, although, from time to time, some extraordinary concerts have taken place in the exquisite surroundings. After a week of sold-out shows at the Boarding House in 1975, Bob Marley and the Wailers moved to the Paramount, where the band vibrated the place heavily and dancers made the balcony sway. The three ladies in LaBelle made their entrance by being lowered from the rafters in an over-the-top 1975 performance. The Village People appearance in 1979 spawned a lobbyful of clones in telephone linemen outfits and motorcycle leathers.

Paramount Theater, an Art Deco landmark. (1973, photographer unknown)

McFadden's Fabulous Ballroom
1933 Broadway, Oakland

A dispirited Benny Goodman pulled into McFadden's one hot August night in 1935. His newly formed big band had taken to the road on its first tour, after being fired from a booking at New York's Roosevelt Grill, and had met utter indifference—and worse—on a grueling string of one-nighters through the Midwest. He was armed with a formidable lineup—Bunny Berigan on trumpet, Jess Stacy on piano, Gene Krupa on drums—and a bristling, blasting book packed with arrangements that Fletcher Henderson wrote for the band's NBC radio "Let's Dance" broadcasts earlier in the year. But the reception his orchestra was getting its first time out was making Goodman think about trying a sweeter, lighter sound, more along the lines of Guy Lombardo. McFadden's, however, was packed with raving, cheering dancers and the following week, at Los Angeles's Palomar Ballroom, he duplicated the response, launching not only the career of the King of Swing, but the entire Swing era.

Continental Club
1658 Twelfth Street, Oakland

Dubbed "the Coliseum of the Oakland blues" by no less distinguished an authority than guitarist George Thorogood, who appeared in a benefit at the huge West Oakland club when he was all but unknown, the Continental Club goes back to the early fifties. Then it was known as Chris' Grill, before being remodeled into the Rhumboogie Club and enlarged again and renamed the Continental sometime in the mid-sixties. B.B. King played the club, as did Otis Redding and the Temptations. For a brief period in the early seventies, bluesman Jimmy McCracklin ran the room, booking major blues acts like T-Bone Walker, Irma Thomas, Big Joe Turner, Big Mama Thornton, and Etta James, although there was to be no blues revival for West Oakland. The large hall is still available on a rental basis.

Earl (Fatha) Hines Home
815 Trestle Glen, Oakland

For the last quarter-century of his life, Earl Hines, one of the cornerstones of jazz piano history, lived quietly in this upscale Diamond Heights neighborhood, traveling the world and performing up until the weekend before his death in 1983.

East Bay

Frenchy's
29097 Mission Boulevard, Hayward

Sly and the Family Stone practically served as the house band at this rough-and-tumble rock club from the band's earliest days right up through *Dance to the Music* in 1968. With ads widely trumpeted on Top 40 radio, the club drew a car crowd from all over the East Bay and remained remote from the provincial social changes taking place in San Francisco and Berkeley at the time. Frenchy's was still home to greasers and hot-rodders, even though the Grateful Dead, in the band's young days as the Warlocks (featuring a first performance by bassist Phil Lesh with the band), played an early gig there.

Brent Mydland Gravesite
Oakmont Cemetery, 2099 Reliez Valley Road, Lafayette

Raised in nearby Concord, keyboardist Brent Mydland, who joined the Grateful Dead in 1979 and played with the band for eleven years until his death in 1990, never entirely escaped the tag of being the "new guy." At the time of his death from a toxic combination of cocaine and morphine, he was separated from his wife and family, a lonely and depressed man. His grave on this sunny hillside is often decorated with homemade signs and offerings from Deadheads paying their respects.

Brent Mydland Gravesite. (1995, photo by David F. Selvin)

Concord Pavilion

2000 Kirker Pass Road, Concord

Carl Jefferson ran Concord's largest Lincoln-Mercury dealership, but his real love was always jazz. He began a small jazz festival in a city park in 1968 and, by the fourth year, was selling out three consecutive weekends by presenting jazz greats Ella Fitzgerald, Oscar Peterson, and Benny Goodman. A tireless civic booster, Jefferson convinced the town leaders to come up with $4.5 million to build an open-air amphitheater. Henry Mancini and Sarah Vaughan presided over the 1975 opening concert. In 1985, Bill Graham Presents signed a deal to book the facility. Presenting about sixty shows a year, Concord has played host to a parade of entertainers, from Frank Sinatra to Dire Straits, Bette Midler to Eric Clapton, Rod Stewart to Reba McEntire. Swedish pop-rockers Abba played the group's only Northern California concert at the Pavilion. Flying home from a Huey Lewis and the News concert here, promoter Bill Graham and two others died in a helicopter crash in October 1991.

Concord Pavilion.
(1977, photographer
unknown)

East Bay

Altamont Speedway
17001 Midway Road, Livermore

A dilapidated track is visible from the freeway as drivers round the interchange that connects 580 East with Interstate 5 South, marking the site of a car and motorcycle raceway in business since the forties. The operation was on the verge of financial collapse when the Rolling Stones announced plans for a free concert in Golden Gate Park to cap the band's triumphant 1969 U.S. tour. When the city refused to grant a permit for such an unwieldly event, no site had been located five days before the scheduled concert. Sear's Point Raceway volunteered and a stage was under construction when the Sonoma County facility's corporate parent, Filmways Corporation, demanded the film rights to the documentary movie being made of the concert. With less than twenty-four hours before the start of the concert, the Stones hired lawyer Melvin Belli to handle negotiations with Filmways. Belli fielded a chance phone call from Dick Carter, manager of the Altamont track. Carter wanted nothing more than the publicity for his beleaguered raceway, and helicopters began ferrying staging and sound equipment to the remote location in the barren hills of the East Bay.

As vividly documented in the Maysles brothers' film, *Gimme Shelter,* the events of that December day were nothing short of catastrophic. More than four hundred thousand rock fans made their way to the site, literally abandoning their cars en route, and turning the highway into a parking lot. The Hell's Angels, hired as security guards, rampaged, beating the crowd into submission with pool cues and knocking Jefferson Airplane vocalist Marty Balin unconscious when he jumped into the crowd to try and stop a fight. The Stones waited until after sundown to perform and during "Sympathy for the Devil," a knife-wielding assailant was beaten, stabbed, and stomped to death by the Angels swarming over him, as the Stones performance skittered to a halt and Jagger nervously pleaded for calm.

The Grateful Dead, scheduled to follow the Stones, never played, although the show did boast an extraordinary lineup of Santana, Flying Burrito Brothers, Crosby, Stills, Nash and Young, and the Airplane. The resulting publicity did the track little good, and the site has been fenced off, marked with no trespassing signs, closed now for many years.

North Bay

1

2

Otis Redding's dock ... Moby Grape's bust ...
Bill Graham's crash ... Janis Joplin's rock star
home in the woods ... Aretha Franklin cuts
"Freeway of Love" ... Huey Lewis and the
American Express ... Elvis Costello's favorite
record store ... the first rock festival ...
Rumours, and *Songs in the Key of Life.*

1 Janis Joplin House
2 Village Music

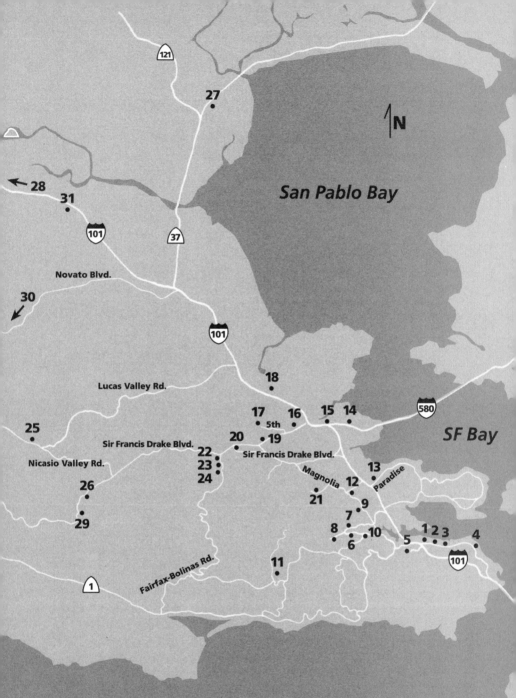

121

27

N

San Pablo Bay

28

31

101

37

Novato Blvd.

30

101

Lucas Valley Rd.

18

25

17   16
5th
20   19

15   14

580

SF Bay

Sir Francis Drake Blvd.

22
23
24

Sir Francis Drake Blvd.

13

Nicasio Valley Rd.

Magnolia

Paradise

26

21

12
9

29

7

8
6

10

1 2 3
5   4

11

101

Fairfax-Bolinas Rd.

1

Pacific Ocean

North Bay

1 The Dock of the Bay,
  Main Dock, Waldo
  Point, Sausalito
2 The Ark, Waldo Point,
  Sausalito
3 The Plant Studios,
  Sausalito
4 The Trident, Sausalito
5 Moby Grape Bust Site,
  Marin City
6 Marty Balin Home,
  Mill Valley
7 Village Music,
  Mill Valley
8 Sweetwater, Mill Valley
9 Grace Slick Home,
  Mill Valley
10 2 A.M. Club, Mill Valley
11 Mountain Theater,
  Mill Valley
12 Masada, Corte Madera

13 Uncle Charlie's,
  Corte Madera
14 Tarpan Studios,
  San Rafael
15 Club Front, San Rafael
16 New George's,
  San Rafael
17 Tom Donahue Gravesite,
  Mt. Tamalpais
  Cemetery, San Rafael
18 Marin Veteran's
  Memorial Auditorium,
  San Rafael
19 Lion's Share,
  San Anselmo
20 The Church,
  San Anselmo
21 Janis Joplin Home,
  Larkspur
22 Caledonia Records,
  Fairfax
23 Sleeping Lady Cafe,
  Fairfax
24 Junktiques, Fairfax
25 The Site, Nicasio

26 Serenity Knolls,
  Forest Knolls
27 Bill Graham Crash Site,
  Hwy. 37, between
  Sears Point and
  Vallejo
28 Inn of the Beginning,
  Cotati
29 Argentina House,
  Lagunitas
30 Mickey Hart Ranch,
  Novato
31 Rancho Olompali,
  Novato

The Musical History Tour

The Dock of the Bay
Main Dock, Waldo Point Harbor, Sausalito

In August 1967, Otis Redding played a six-night engagement at San Francisco's Basin Street West. Road manager Earl (Speedo) Sims remembered that some women discovered Redding's hotel and the soul man decided to move to a more remote location. He and Redding rented a houseboat on the main dock of the Sausalito houseboat community and holed up. Sitting, not on the dock, but inside the houseboat's living room, Redding, under the spell of the recently released Beatles album, *Sergeant Pepper's Lonely Hearts Club Band,* strummed guitar while Speedo beat out the tempo by slapping his hands on his legs, sketching out a song. On his return to Memphis, Redding underwent surgery to remove polyps from his throat, and for some time he couldn't speak above a whisper. When he finally returned to the studio in November, he was spurred by a burst of creative energy, recording more than two dozen new songs in a few weeks. The last song he cut was the new piece that had begun to take shape on that houseboat in the Sausalito harbor, "(Sittin' on the) Dock of the Bay." The next day, he left Memphis for a Midwest swing starting in Cleveland. He left Cleveland for Madison, Wisconsin, but never arrived. His twin-engine Beechcraft crashed into the chilly waters of Lake Monona, just short of his destination. When "Dock of the Bay" was released in January, the record became the first number-one hit of Redding's too-brief career.

The Dock of the Bay inspired the Otis Redding number one hit. (1995, photo by Keta Bill Selvin)

The Sausalito houseboat community practically qualified as an artists' colony during the sixties. Dino Valente wrote "Get Together" while living on the *Becky Thatcher*. Dan Hicks lived on a houseboat and Bill Cosby kept a palatial floating residence berthed there. Bob Dylan spent an evening writing songs on Shel Silverstein's boat. At various times, John Cipollina of Quicksilver Messenger Service and Ramblin' Jack Elliott hung their hats at the docks.

The Ark
Gate Five, Waldo Point Harbor, Sausalito

A giant paddle wheel sunk deep in the mud and the tattered, weather-beaten wheelhouse are all that remains of the *Charles Van Damme,* a ferryboat originally commissioned in 1915 but retired to Sausalito, scuttled on the mudflats, to become Juanita's Galley, a noted eccentric bar presided over by the redoubtable, muumuu-draped Juanita Musson. Rechristened The Ark after Musson left for Sonoma, the club became a focal point of the burgeoning folk scene in the early sixties, a second home to unknowns like David Crosby and Dino Valente. Before going out of business permanently, the club switched to rock and a Canadian band called The Sparrow served a lengthy residency in 1966, before moving to Los Angeles and changing its name to Steppenwolf. Opening the shows for The Sparrow was a fresh, new band called Moby Grape playing its first public engagements. Buffalo Springfield members Stephen Stills and Neil Young used to hang out and occasionally jam with the three-guitar band, and Columbia Records staff producer David Rubinson, in town to work with The Sparrow, caught the Grape and arranged to sign them.

The Plant Studios
2200 Bridgeway, Sausalito

More than simply the place where Fleetwood Mac recorded *Rumours,* Huey Lewis and the News cut *Sports,* or Stevie Wonder did *Songs In the Key of Life,* the Plant is the Bay Area's most historic recording facility. When Gary Kellgren and Chris Stone, who already operated highly successful record plants in Los Angeles and New York, opened the Sausalito site with an extravagant party on Halloween 1972, John and Yoko came dressed as trees and Buddy Miles was the opening act. When Sly Stone began recording at the wood-shingled building on the side street below Sausalito's busiest thoroughfare, he actually moved in—sleeping, eating, bathing, literally living in the studio.

The studio hummed with activity. America, Stephen Stills, Van Morrison, Yes, and Marvin Gaye were among the clientele. When Kellgren died in a swimming pool accident in 1977, his partner Stone lost interest in the business, and sold the Marin County operation to Laurie Nechochea, a young wheelchairbound woman who used her abundant malpractice settlement to ingratiate herself into the rock world. Her trust administrators soon put a stop to that, forcing her to sell the studio, its name now shortened to The Plant. She died less than a year later at age twenty-three.

The new owner, Stanley Jacox, a Sacramento-based entrepreneur, hired Stax/Volt staffer Jim Gaines as general manager. John Fogerty was their first client, cutting what became his miraculous comeback album, *Centerfield*. Heart cut "These Dreams" here. At one point, the three rooms were booked simultaneously by Huey Lewis and the News, Jefferson Starship, and Journey. But when Jacox was arrested for drug trafficking and tax evasion charges, federal agents swooped down on The Plant, impounding the entire facility and actually operating the studio until it could be sold (wags called the place Club Fed during that period).

In 1986, Bob Skye and Arne Frager became the new owners and the place continued to flourish. Clients including Van Morrison, Santana, Sammy Hagar, and Kenny G booked time. Producer Walter Afanasieff brought in artists like Mariah Carey, Michael Bolton, and Luther Vandross. He cut the Peabo Bryson/Celine Dion duet for *Beauty and the Beast* there. Metallica edited and mixed the band's 1994 live album at the studio, and Booker T. Jones rented a room in the studio for his exclusive personal use the first year he lived in the Bay Area.

The Trident

558 Bridgeway, Sausalito

The ultimate hip restaurant in the sixties, boasting decent food, colorful waitresses, and an unparalleled waterfront view, the Trident was opened in 1961 by Frank Werber, manager of the Kingston Trio. The only music the bistro ever featured was jazz, and pianists Denny Zeitlin and Bill Evans both cut live albums at the fashionable bayside club. Trumpeter Chet Baker was playing the room in 1968 when a dope deal went bad in San Francisco and Baker was beaten to a bloody pulp, including having his two front teeth broken out, a disastrous injury to the trumpet player who never fully recovered. Bill Graham closed the place for an epic party to honor the Rolling Stones after the band's triumphant 1972 Winterland performances. Werber eventually lost interest and sold the enterprise in 1980, keeping the name, although the room and the view still remain.

Moby Grape Bust Site
fire trail off the end of Donahue Street, Marin City

The night in May 1967 began with a jubilant record-release party at the Avalon Ballroom. The scent of orchids flown in from Hawaii by the record company filled the air. Moby Grape wine was served. Janis Joplin sang a couple of numbers with the band. The group's first album had been launched in gala style, but the musicians weren't ready to stop the party. Police discovered Jerry Miller, Skip Spence, and Peter Lewis in a borrowed T-Bird parked on this well-known lover's lane, with three underage women, Spence without his pants and Miller with a partly smoked joint in his pocket. Newspapers splashed the scandal across the country the following day, beginning the long, slow unraveling of one of San Francisco's most promising groups ever.

Marty Balin Home
180 E. Blithedale, Mill Valley

A Mill Valley landmark ever since the Jefferson Airplane vocalist built the unusual roof under the sway of pyramid power in the seventies, the house sits on the main avenue leading to downtown Mill Valley and is hard to miss, even if it is hidden behind shrubbery and trees. Balin bought the place more than twenty-five years ago in the first flush of his success and has maintained his local residence here, even after moving to Florida several years ago.

Village Music
9 E. Blithedale, Mill Valley

As much museum as record store, Village Music is Marin County's record store to the stars. Elvis Costello always manages to stop by when he passes through town. Mick Jagger stocked up on Afro-pop before heading off on the 1981 Rolling Stones tour. All the local rockers have shopped there since its 1968 opening. Owner John Goddard has covered the walls with his amazing collection of memorabilia—a 1955 Faron Young poster with the opening act, Elvis Presley, a Robert Johnson 78 r.p.m. record, John Cipollina's guitar.

Sweetwater

153 Throckmorton, Mill Valley

Owner Jeannie Patterson plays den mother to so many musicians that they can't resist working her tiny club. Since the downtown Mill Valley bar is the neighborhood tavern for many rock musicians, she has become an unofficial hostess of the scene since the club opened in the late seventies. John Lee Hooker drives up from his Redwood City home to work the room. He shot a BBC documentary at the one hundred-seat club with guests Bonnie Raitt, Ry Cooder, Albert Collins, and Robert Cray. Carlos Santana has brought his full band onto the postage-stamp-size stage. Sammy Hagar rented the place for a private Halloween party (and came dressed as Jimi Hendrix) and, on another occasion, joined the fray with Nick Gravenites, Maria Muldaur, and Clarence Clemons. Bill Graham used to routinely stop off for a toddy on his way home. Mark Knopfler of Dire Straits joined one of his role models, J.J. Cale, onstage at the club and George Thorogood sat in with John Hammond. Huey Lewis and the News performed at the wake for the bass player's mother at the small club. Hot Tuna recorded a pair of CDs live at the club in 1992. Village Music's John Goddard has hosted a number of memorable parties at the club featuring many of the musicians he most loves—Charles Brown, Jimmy Scott, Ry Cooder, NRBQ, Richard Berry, Carla Thomas, Hank Ballard and the Midnighters— although his crowning moment came when he brought together on the same stage Elvis Costello, Jerry Garcia, and Elvis Presley's guitar player, James Burton.

Sweetwater, Marin rockers' favorite club. (1995, photo by Keta Bill Selvin)

Grace Slick Home

18 Escalon, Mill Valley

When a 1993 fire destroyed her Mill Valley hillside home of many years, Jefferson Airplane singer Grace Slick was so dispirited that she moved to Los Angeles after a lifetime of living in the Bay Area. Although the house itself was fully rebuilt, the blaze took a massive collection of dolls that had previously crowded every available ledge and nook of the dwelling.

2 A.M. Club

Miller Avenue at Monfort Street, Mill Valley

This slightly seedy, well-seasoned hangout was immortalized on the cover of the Huey Lewis and the News album *Sports*. The bar used to boast a gold-album award for the famous record hanging on its walls.

Mountain Theater

off E. Ridgecrest Boulevard, Mount Tamalpais, Mill Valley

The weekend prior to the historic 1967 Monterey Pop Festival, a much less-publicized rock festival took place at the top of Mount Tam. The Magic Mountain Music Festival and Fantasy Fair, in fact, may have been the first rock festival ever. Produced by one of the town's leading Top 40 disc jockeys as a benefit for Hunter's Point child-care centers, the show was attended by more than fifteen thousand people over two days. The road leading up Mt. Tam was closed for the duration and ticket-holders were brought to the site by bus from the foot of the mountain. Hell's Angels provided transportation for some of the groups. Among those appearing were Jefferson Airplane, Fifth Dimension, The Byrds, Canned Heat, Country Joe and the Fish, Dionne Warwick, and The Doors, whose lead vocalist, Jim Morrison, fell off the stage during his performance while swinging drunkenly on a lighting post.

Masada

800 Corte Madera Avenue, Corte Madera

Off the road behind the gate at the top of the hill overlooking Mill Valley, producer Bill Graham lived in a large home on well-kept grounds. Originally owned by famed trial lawyer Jake Erlich, Graham bought the house for a relatively modest $700,000 in 1978. After his death in 1991, the estate sold the property for almost $6 million, the largest real estate deal in southern Marin County history at the time. It was a bachelor's mansion, a ranch-style house with one bedroom and a grand dining room where Graham entertained rock royalty and business associates regularly. He kept large props from Grateful Dead concerts and Live Aid, the 1985 global telethon he helped stage, beside the winding road leading up to the house, which were moved to the backstage area at Shoreline Amphitheater after his death.

Uncle Charlie's
5625 Paradise Drive, Corte Madera

Hanging around after his band Clover dissolved after returning from England in 1979, vocalist Huey Lewis put a loose-knit band together to play after Monday night football games at this bar in a suburban shopping center. He used the rhythm section from another defunct Marin County group called Soundhole and the keyboard player from Clover, switching off guitarists as if he were auditioning musicians. After finding one he liked, the group went into the studio and recorded a demo tape under the name Huey Lewis and the American Express. The tape attracted the interest of Pablo Cruise's manager and a showcase for the band was arranged opening for Van Morrison at the Old Waldorf. After no more than two official live appearances, the band landed a recording contract, changed its name to avoid a possible lawsuit, and never returned to Uncle Charlie's, which closed for good a few years later.

Tarpan Studios
1925 Francisco Boulevard, San Rafael

This unlikely looking facade in an industrial park houses a genuine hit factory, the Motown of Marin, home to Grammy-winning producer Narada Michael Walden. In the well-equipped studio, he has cut hit records with Aretha Franklin, Whitney Houston, Jefferson Starship, Mariah Carey, Eddie Murphy, Kenny G, and others. Lionel Richie once visited the facility, preparatory to recording sessions that never actually took place. Daryl Hannah brought her then-boyfriend Jackson Browne with her when she came to sing background vocals on a Clarence Clemons solo record, "You're a Friend of Mine."

Club Front

20 Front Street, San Rafael

Serving as the rehearsal hall and general band headquarters for the Grateful
Dead since the mid-seventies, this modest warehouse was converted into a
recording studio that the band whimsically dubbed Club Front. The Dead
album, *Shakedown Street,* produced by Lowell George of Little Feat, and the
Jerry Garcia Band album, *Cats Under the Stars,* were both recorded here in
1978, as was the 1980 Dead album, *Go to Heaven.*

New George's

842 Fourth Street, San Rafael

Since Uncle Charlie's closed, New George's has reigned as the sole major
rock club in Marin County, not only drawing out-of-town acts but local bands
looking for a club date in the area. With local rock stars dropping by from time
to time to see their favorite acts, it's not unusual to catch such sights as Carlos
Santana sitting in with the Fabulous Thunderbirds.

Tom Donahue Gravesite

Mt. Tamalpais Cemetery, 2500 Fifth Street, San Rafael

The father of FM radio was cremated and his ashes interred in this Marin
County cemetery. Donahue died in 1975 of a massive heart attack during a
marathon backgammon game, where he was ingesting his typical lion's share
of favorite alkaloids, leaving behind plans to vacate his beloved KSAN for a new
radio station, with filmmaker Francis Ford Coppola providing the funding.
A onetime Top 40 kingpin on KYA who produced rock concerts at the Cow
Palace and elsewhere (including the final public performance by the Beatles at
Candlestick Park in 1966), Donahue was a giant in a field of midgets. He owned
a record company, a nightclub, and a few racehorses. The four hundred-fifty
pounder who called himself "Big Daddy" took over the twenty-four-hour oper-
ations of KMPX-FM in June 1967 and essentially invented modern rock radio.
He took the entire staff to KSAN in the wake of a strike the following year.
After his death, radio in San Francisco was never the same.

Marin Veteran's Memorial Auditorium
Marin County Civic Center, Avenue of the Flags, San Rafael

Designed carefully to fit in with the rest of the Frank Lloyd Wright-designed civic center, the Marin Veteran's Memorial Auditorium has served as a journeyman community theater since opening night in 1971. Artists who have appeared at the two thousand-seat hall include Alan Alda, Cary Grant, Duke Ellington, Walter Cronkite, the Vienna Boys Choir, Joel Grey, Dolly Parton, Jay Leno, Rich Little, James Taylor, the Peking Acrobats, Ray Charles, Marcel Marceau, and Huey Lewis and the News. But the room's real role in Bay Area music history came when it settled a long-standing argument and broke a stalemate in the ranks of the Grateful Dead. The band, which never does anything without a unanimous vote, did not release a new album for a crucial seven years, while the band's audience grew exponentially and the musicians themselves debated the validity of recording. One member held out for his beliefs that the recording studio was simply too sterile an environment in which to create music. Eventually someone suggested that the group rent the Marin Veteran's Hall, convert it to a recording studio, and record the basic tracks to a new album without the audience. That broke the standoff, and the band was able to commit to tape the songs that became the 1987 release, *In the Dark,* the biggest-selling album in the Dead's long history.

Lion's Share
60 Red Hill Avenue, San Anselmo

Operated by Mike Considine, son of a famous newspaper columnist, the Lion's Share opened at the Red Hill Avenue site in fall 1969, after the original Sausalito Lion's Share, a folk spot that started in early 1966 on a $300 investment, burned down. Shel Silverstein was the first attraction at the reopened club. For the next four years, the small club served as rumpus room to the Marin County music scene, featuring Van Morrison, various configurations of the Dead, Jesse Colin Young, plus whoever was around. Clover, the band Huey Lewis started with, and the Sons of Champlin must have played a hundred Lion's Share dates between them. When Janis Joplin died and left a small sum of money to throw a party in her memory, the wake was held at the Lion's Share, where musicians could always get in for $1.

The Church

1405 San Anselmo Avenue, San Anselmo

A popular rehearsal hall for Marin County bands since the sixties, this former place of worship, partly owned by Marty Balin of the Jefferson Airplane, has watched the famous, nearly famous, and entirely unknown march through its doors for more than a quarter century. The Sons of Champlin, who were head-quartered on the premises for years, recorded their most rare album, *Seeds and Stems*, at The Church.

Janis Joplin Home

380 West Baltimore Avenue, Larkspur

Joplin claimed this woodsy, redwood-paneled house on a shady cul-de-sac as the rightful home of a Marin County rock star. Jerry Garcia and Mountain Girl lived across the creek running through the backyard. The sliding glass doors brought the redwood forest into the spacious high-beamed living room, which Joplin decorated with Oriental rugs and Victorian furniture. The house had originally belonged to a dentist and his family, but Joplin moved in with a live-in housekeeper, a dog, and a steady procession of friends. Her housewarming party in December 1969 was one righteous bash, a decadent decathalon where Joplin ended up shooting dope in the bedroom with her girlfriend and Mike Bloomfield, while drunken party guests staggered blindly around the redwoods outside. She spent the last year of her life living in this rustic serenity, sharing the house in her final months with a new boyfriend before she succumbed to a fatal heroin overdose while staying at the Landmark Motel in Hollywood during recording sessions for her new album.

Janis Joplin's house, a hippie manor befitting her new rock star status. (1970, photo by Greg Peterson)

Caledonia Records
44 Bolinas Road, Fairfax

While located in Marin County in the early seventies, Van Morrison moved his parents over from Ireland to live near him and installed them in this record store for employment in "downtown" Fairfax. After his father died in the late seventies, his mother closed the store and returned to Ireland. Morrison followed her a few years later.

Sleeping Lady Cafe
58 Bolinas Road, Fairfax

The original macrobiotic nightclub, the Sleeping Lady refused to allow smoking long before that prohibition became fashionable. Peter Tork of The Monkees worked in the kitchen and sang in the Fairfax Street Choir, a kind of hippie glee club that used to play at the organic nightclub. A reggae band called the Tazmanian Devils became something of a minor phenomenon through their appearances at the club in the seventies, but when Warner Brothers executives took the company jet up to attend an album release party at the Lady, the brass spent much of the time standing on the sidewalk smoking cigarettes. Devils producer Erik Jacobsen, who had supervised all the hit records by the Lovin' Spoonful, eventually found his niche as producer of Chris Isaak.

Junktiques
341 Bolinas Road, Fairfax

After spending the day driving around fruitlessly looking for possible sites, photographer Jim Marshall and the members of Moby Grape spotted this daffy antique store/junk shop and made one last stab at taking an album cover photograph for the band's classic 1967 debut. Borrowing some props from the store, Marshall arrayed his subjects on the old boardwalk in front and clicked off one roll. Drummer Don Stevenson was irritated enough to express himself by slyly extending his middle finger while he held a washboard. Columbia Records only noticed the offensive gesture after the fact and airbrushed the digit out of existence on later printings. The building was demolished long ago and owner Sonia Birmingham relocated her store to Petaluma.

The Site
Lucas Valley Road, Nicasio

This exquisite studio is allergic to publicity. Even the exact location, down the road from George Lucas's Skywalker Ranch, is a closely guarded secret. In fact, many of the album credits for the studio place it in San Rafael, where the owners keep a post-office box. But in this bucolic setting, artists such as Linda Ronstadt and Booker T. and the MGs have recorded recent albums. Pearl Jam recorded *Vs.* at this remote location. When Keith Richards took over the studio to record a solo album, he ordered the panoramic view from the studio's picture window covered with tin foil, the better to accommodate his vampire schedule.

Serenity Knolls Treatment Center
145 Tamal Road, Forest Knolls

At the bottom of a dead-end road in the dark early morning hours of August 9, 1995, a night nurse making her rounds discovered a patient at this rustic drug treatment center had stopped breathing. She summoned paramedics and after they failed to revive him, the sheriff was notified. Death erased the anonymity central to the precepts of 12-Step programs practiced at places like Serenity Knolls because the patient was Jerry Garcia.

The Grateful Dead guitarist had driven himself to the inexpensive, unpretentious lodge in the woods two days earlier, after bailing out of a stay at the more uptown Betty Ford Center outside Palm Springs two weeks before. Fighting a heroin addiction that had vexed him for years, Garcia succumbed to a heart attack brought on in part due to his weight problems, bad diet, and diabetic condition. His private funeral was held three days later at St. Stephens Church in Belvedere, and the Deadheads convened that weekend at the Polo Fields in Golden Gate Park. His ashes were scattered at sea.

Bill Graham Crash Site
Highway 37 between Sears Point and Vallejo

As the highway passes Napa Creek, power lines cross the highway, rising to a giant tower more than two hundred feet high. On a stormy night in October 1991, Bill Graham, his girlfriend, and pilot were returning home from a Huey Lewis and the News concert at the Concord Pavilion when their helicopter exploded in a ball of fire when it hit the uppermost part of the tower, killing all three instantly. The pilot was speaking to airport traffic controllers just minutes before the crash about the lack of warning lights on utility towers in the area. "You always have to wait until somebody gets hurt or killed before they do anything," he said. Graham's sons later sued PG&E for violating FAA regulations about unmarked towers over a certain height, but the tower remains in place.

Inn of the Beginning
8201 Old Redwood Highway, Cotati

From 1968 through 1982, this funky beer bar brought rock to Sonoma County. All the local bands passed through the rustic club next door to the biker bar. Van Morrison booked dates a few hours before playing them. Neil Young and Crazy Horse called one afternoon in 1975 and turned up to play that night. Rosanne Cash made her public performance debut at the out-of-the-way showcase in 1979. Bronze Hog was a rock band that played the club virtually throughout its entire history and was never known outside Cotati. Kate Wolf was a folksinger who used to show up every Sunday at the free folk night. David Bromberg once dropped by to hear a couple of Irish players and, when he saw the audience of about one dozen, he suggested the musicians get off the stage, pulled the chairs into a circle, got his guitar and sat down to jam the night away. When lease problems arose, owner Mark Bronstein deserted the bar for the larger Cotati Cabaret across the street. But in 1993, after the room stood empty for ten years, someone reopened the club, booking acoustic music four or five nights a week to complement the coffeehouse/microbrewery atmosphere of the new Inn.

Argentina House
1 Spring Road, Lagunitas

During most of 1966, Big Brother and the Holding Company lived together communally at this old house hidden in the woods. Someone had painted the word "Argentina" on the propane tank beside the road leading up to the house, giving the place its name. After Big Brother vacated the premises in favor of residency in the Haight-Ashbury, the Sons of Champlin took over the property, also referred to as Teddy Roosevelt's hunting lodge because the ex-president was said to have once stayed there on a hunting trip. When the Sons eventually left the ramshackle house, the band's then-manager, Walter Haas, son of the Levi's magnate and eventually president of the Oakland A's baseball team, assumed ownership and remodeled the house into a showplace.

Mickey Hart Ranch

2495 S. Novato Boulevard, Novato

When drummer Mickey Hart of the Grateful Dead left the Haight-Ashbury and rented this northern Marin County ranch, the weathered barn on the premises became the band's unofficial rehearsal hall, meeting room, and even recording studio. The New Riders of the Purple Sage formed in the barn, with longtime Jerry Garcia buddy David Nelson hooking up with Hart, Garcia, and bassist Phil Lesh to start the Dead country-and-western offshoot. Hart's father, Lenny Hart, delivered something of a sermon to the band concerning financial responsibilities—a fact of life the musicians had chosen to ignore as much as possible—in the barn that led to his taking a position as manager of the band. His stealing tens of thousands of dollars from the group's bank accounts led to his imprisonment and his son quitting the band in 1970. Hart stayed on the ranch, recording his own solo album, *Rolling Thunder,* on the site. Long after he moved on, the buildings burned down and the land became part of a state park.

Rancho Olompali

Olompali State Park, Novato

On the site of a nineteenth-century adobe village and the only battle in the 1884 Bear Flag revolt, a twenty-six-room ranch house that doubled as a school for disturbed youth became the summer home of the Grateful Dead in 1966. The parties the band held here are the stuff of legend—naked dancers, outdoor performances, people thrown in the pool, drugs, sex, and other forms of merriment—and drew virtually every member of the nascent San Francisco rock scene, establishing Marin County as a satellite territory to the Haight-Ashbury. The house was subsequently taken over by a hippie commune calling itself the Chosen Family, who were living there when it burned to the ground in 1969. Added to the state's list of historic places in 1972, the land has since been deeded over to serve as a state park.

7

South Bay

The Warlocks and the early Grateful Dead ...
Joan Baez, high school folksinger ... Tower
of Power murder case ... the Doobie Brothers
at biker bars ... the forming of The Eagles ...
Tony Orlando and Marvin Gaye return to the
stage ... Neil Young country ... Monterey
Pop Festival ... *Brisbane Bop*

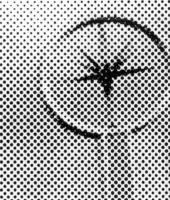

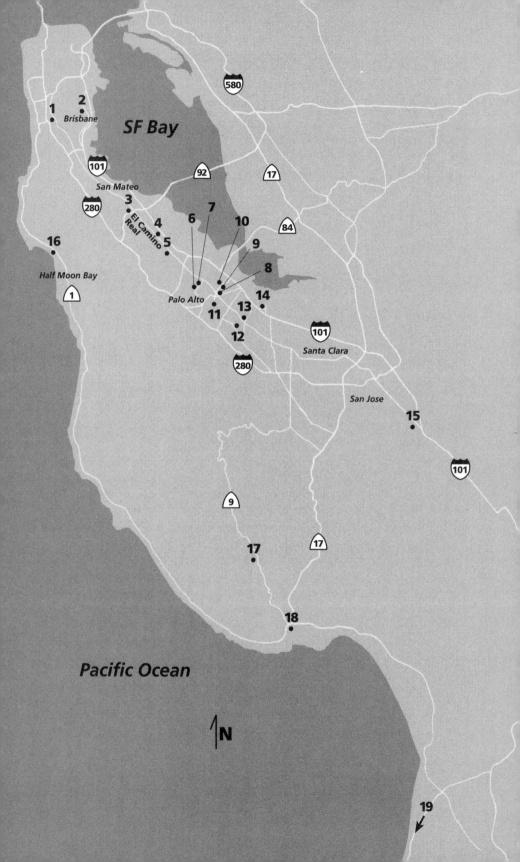

SF Bay

580

1

2

Brisbane

101

San Mateo

92

17

3

280

El Camino Real

4

6

7

10

9

84

5

8

16

Half Moon Bay

1

Palo Alto

11

13

14

12

101

280

Santa Clara

San Jose

15

101

9

17

17

18

Pacific Ocean

19

N

South Bay

The Musical History Tour

Bill Graham Gravesite

Eternal Home Cemetery, 1051 El Camino Real, Colma

In an unlikely setting close to the roar of traffic from the busy street nearby, a black marble headstone marks the final resting place of concert producer Bill Graham, who died in a fiery helicopter crash in October 1991. Born Wolfgang Wolodia Grajonza in Berlin, Germany, on January 8, 1931, Graham escaped the Nazis on a torturous walk across France. Sixty-three children started that walk; all but eleven died, including his sister. After an aimless professional path led him through stints as a soldier, waiter in the Catskills, cab driver, and amateur actor, Graham arrived in San Francisco to work as an office manager. He fell back into the theater world as business manager of the perennially beleaguered S.F. Mime Troupe and, by throwing a 1965 benefit concert to raise money for the troupe's legal defense fund, found his calling. From the Fillmore Auditorium to the worldwide broadcast of Live Aid, Graham became the single most dominant figure in rock concert promotion. A restless, driven spirit always looking for new worlds to conquer and new bands to produce, he was an indomitable influence on the rock music scene from almost the moment he set foot in it.

Bill Graham Gravesite.
(1995, photo by Keta
Bill Selvin)

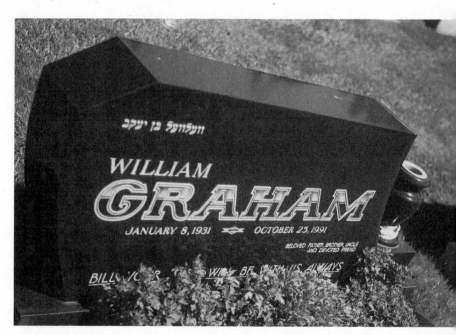

DeMarco's 23 Club

23 Visitacion Avenue, Brisbane

DeMarco's made the Guinness Book of Records in the early seventies when the historic country-and-western club sponsored a barbecue, in which seven buffaloes were roasted at once. Johnny DeMarco moved to this city between the railroad tracks from Louisiana in 1941. When he died of cancer in 1975, city hall was closed in mourning. DeMarco made his nightclub a regular stop on the country-and-western circuit for Hank Snow, Ernest Tubb, Bob Wills, and Lefty Frizell. The faded, dusty photos that line the walls testify to the procession of country music royalty that passed through the doors in the fifties and sixties. Live recordings made at the club in the early sixties by the swinging house band, Jimmy Rivers and the Cherokees, were released some twenty years later on the Western Records label under the title *Brisbane Bop*.

Pacific Recorders

1737 S. El Camino Real, San Mateo

An essential studio in the early days of the San Francisco rock scene, Pacific Recorders was the first sixteen-track studio in the area. The Grateful Dead recorded *Aoxomoxa* here and Santana cut the group's classic first album at the Peninsula studio, where the band also recorded a lot of early demo sessions, as did the Doobie Brothers. Long out of business, the building was most recently occupied by a hot-tub retailer.

Circle Star Theater

1717 Industrial Road, San Carlos

An aberration of the sixties, theaters-in-the-round were supposed to be popular because the back row would still be relatively close to the stage in a room that seated more than three thousand people. What such a configuration really meant is that all seats were equally bad. Wide-mouthed comedian Joe E. Brown attended the groundbreaking ceremonies here and *My Fair Lady* was the opening attraction in October 1964. Investors included Juliet Prowse, Nat King Cole, Jimmy Durante, and other show biz figures, along with producers Sammy Lewis and Danny Dare, who built a similar operation in Anaheim. Nat King Cole played his final performance at the theater, discovering his fatal lung cancer during the 1964 engagement. The following year, a withered and wasted Judy Garland played an evening show on the same day the Beatles appeared some miles up the freeway at the Cow Palace. In between short runs of touring musicals during the first few seasons, the theater hosted performances by Jimmy Durante, the Dave Clark Five, Louis Armstrong, Mahalia Jackson, Beach Boys, and "Shindig '65," a collection of teen rockers from the popular TV show. Within four years, the producers had run the $2.5 million investment aground. With new financing, the theater reopened for nine months the following year, but foundered again.

In 1971, Mill Run Entertainment of Chicago took over the building's management and reopened the theater with Sammy Davis Jr. as the attraction. The first season's lineup established the basic booking policy: Connie Francis, Frank Sinatra, Tony Bennett, Dionne Warwick, Liberace, Glen Campbell, Shecky Greene, Don Rickles, Sergio Franchi, and Brasil '66. Over the years, the theater presented a laundry list of soul and country acts, staying close to the mainstream pop music that was the operation's main trade.

Neil Diamond passed through the Circle Star in 1972 on his way, in the words of comedian Albert Brooks, "to pricing himself out of the business." The Jackson Five worked the circular stage in 1974. *Laugh-In* comic Lily Tomlin, opening for soul singer Bill Withers, spun herself on a bar stool rather than use the motorized stage.

Tony Orlando made his post-Dawn solo debut in 1977 after coming back from a complete breakdown. Richard Pryor returned to performing (after burning himself up) in a 1981 last-minute booking, a warm-up one week before filming *Live on Sunset Strip*. Julio Iglesias, unknown to Anglo audiences at the time, made his first English-only appearance in 1983, admonishing the all-Hispanic audience not to speak Spanish. Two weeks later, Marvin Gaye played his first concert anywhere in four years here, after returning from European exile on the heels of his comeback hit, "Sexual Healing."

In 1986, after three years of ownership by eccentric San Diego dentist Dr. Leonard Bloom, the property went into receivership and, although briefly revived by Peninsula car dealer Jim Birney, the theater operation never regained its footing and has been closed since 1993.

Drum City

894 Laurel Street, San Carlos

As a child, Mickey Hart never knew his father. Lenny Hart left home when the boy was still a child and all he left behind was a pair of rosewood drumsticks. Years later, when young Hart was serving in the Drums and Bugle Corps, he met up with his long-lost father, a lifelong drummer who was working at the time for a savings and loan in Los Angeles. A few years later, after losing touch again, Hart mustered out of the Air Force and settled in New York to begin a career as a professional musician. He received a letter from his father inviting him to move to California and work in the music store he had opened in San Carlos. Hart accepted the invitation and reignited his father's old love of drumming. Within months, the store had been renamed Drum City and was wall-to-wall drums. All went along swimmingly until one night when Mickey Hart went to the Straight Theater to sit in with the Grateful Dead. He never returned to his father's store.

The Chateau
838 Santa Cruz Avenue, Menlo Park

A rambling house of disorder rented by a handful of beatnik folk musicians, this long-gone edifice was the birthplace of the Grateful Dead. Banjo player Jerry Garcia lived here with Robert Hunter, later the band's lyricist, who participated in notorious experiments with LSD and other psychedelic materials conducted by the nearby Veteran's Hospital. Blues singer Ron McKernan, who called himself Pigpen, used to visit. The Chateau brought together the original cast of characters that spawned the Grateful Dead.

Magoo's Pizza Parlor
639 Santa Cruz Avenue, Menlo Park

In May 1965, the Warlocks played three Saturday nights at this tiny hole-in-the-wall, a suds and pizza joint for the campus crowd, which effectively introduced the new group to public performances. Although Dana Morgan Jr. still played bass with the band, Phil Lesh, an acquaintance of guitarist Jerry Garcia's, and a classically trained trumpeter who wanted to learn to play electric bass, stopped by to check out the band and, by the next month, had joined the group.

Phil Lesh Home
1012 High Street, Palo Alto

It was at Lesh's house late in 1965 where the members of the Warlocks, thumbing through an encyclopedia, stumbled across the reference to "the grateful dead" and decided to change the band's name. The first time the group appeared under the name was the second Mime Troupe benefit Bill Graham threw in December 1965. Graham insisted on putting "Formerly the Warlocks" on posters for the event.

St. Michael's Alley
436 University Avenue, Palo Alto

Focal point of the active Peninsula folk scene in the sixties, St. Michael's Alley was the starting place for Palo Alto high school student Joan Baez. "She used to drive me crazy," said owner Vernon Gates. "Once she'd start singing, she'd never stop. People would just sit there listening, wouldn't buy anything." Jerry Garcia used to work in Swain's Music Store across the street and he and future Grateful Dead lyricist Robert Hunter tried out their Jerry and Bob act on the St. Michael's stage. Gates closed the place in 1966, but reopened at 800 Emerson Street in 1973, where he continued to present live music every night until he retired in 1994.

Dana Morgan Music
534 Bryant Street, Palo Alto

High school student Bob Weir and a friend walked by the Palo Alto music store early New Year's Eve 1963 and heard music coming from inside. They knocked on the door and Jerry Garcia, a guitar teacher at the store haplessly waiting for his students, answered. Since no guitar students were going to show up on New Year's Eve, they were invited in and spent the evening jamming on instruments borrowed from the store. The store's owner loaned equipment to the musicians who formed the first edition of the band that became the Grateful Dead (first called the Warlocks), and his son, Dana Morgan Jr., played bass, until his attendance at rehearsals and gigs grew problematic.

Frost Amphitheater
Stanford University, Palo Alto

Named for alumnus Laurence Frost (Class of '32), this beautiful if infrequently used amphitheater in the center of the Stanford campus has been the site of some notable shows by the Grateful Dead, Eric Clapton, and The Band.

Pigpen Gravesite
Alta Mesa Cemetery, 695 Arastradero Road, Palo Alto

In many ways the soul of the early Grateful Dead, Ron (Pigpen) McKernan died alone in his Corte Madera home March 8, 1973, at the age of twenty-seven. His body was discovered by a neighbor. His family held a Roman Catholic funeral at Daphne Funerals in Marin, with the bluesman laid out in cowboy hat and leather jacket with a skull patch in an open casket. His tombstone features the familiar skull with the lightning bolt and the inscription "Pigpen was and is now forever one of the Grateful Dead."

Chuck's Cellar
4926 El Camino Real, Los Altos

A rather typical stop on the steak and lobster circuit, Chuck's Cellar featured singer-songwriter types on the folkie side through most of the seventies. James Lee Reeves sometimes seemed as if he were making his entire living at the club, and John Stewart often qualified as a major star at the suburban spot. But, oddly enough, the club was the site of a little-known historic rock event one weekend in 1971, when Linda Ronstadt was the headliner. To play the date, she had to put together a backup band. Her producer suggested some itinerant musicians: a bassist with Rick Nelson, a drummer from a band called Shiloh, and another guitarist from a group named Longbranch Pennywhistle. The three musicians liked playing together so well that they decided to see if they could work out something more permanent, so Randy Meisner, Don Henley, and Glenn Frey formed The Eagles.

Shoreline Amphitheatre
1 Amphitheatre Parkway, Mountain View

Bill Graham conceived, built, and opened this twenty thousand-capacity open-air amphitheater in October 1986, a $20 million venture in partnership with a handful of investors, including Apple computer magnate Steve Wozniak, who maintains a private box for all Shoreline concerts. In addition to a regular series of concerts from spring through late fall, the theater has become renowned as the annual setting for Neil Young's Bridge School benefit. Young has inveigled a staggering array of his music colleagues into appearing in the acoustic showcase, including Bruce Springsteen, Elton John, Elvis Costello, Pearl Jam, Simon and Garfunkel, Tom Petty, Don Henley, and many others.

Edenvale Elementary School
285 Azucar Street, San Jose

After eluding authorities for two days after a triple murder in the Santa Cruz mountains, Tower of Power lead vocalist Rick Stevens was run down by dozens of police cars, while a police helicopter hovered overhead, and surrendered at gunpoint in a school playground that had been filled with children less than fifteen minutes earlier in February 1976. After killing two drug dealers to whom he owed $3,000 two nights before, Stevens, who had taken refuge at the South San Jose home of an old friend, shot and killed his friend, tied up his friend's girlfriend with a phone cord, and stole his Cadillac. He briefly lost the police pursuit that picked him up cruising north on Highway 101 and then on the winding roads leading to Skyway Drive. He parked the Cadillac by the side of the road, exchanged a few words with a motorcyclist practicing sharp turns on the hillside, snorted a pile of cocaine off the palm of his hand, and headed down the hillside to the school yard. When a motorcycle officer approached him with his gun drawn, Stevens looked nonplussed. "Hey, man," he said, "what's the hassle?" Stevens, who sang Tower of Power staples such as "Sparkling in the Sand," "Down to the Nightclub," and "You're Still a Young Man," was eventually sentenced to life imprisonment for the three murders.

Miramar Beach Inn
131 Mirada Road, Half Moon Bay

A classic coastal roadhouse a couple of hundred yards off Highway 1 built more than eighty years ago, the Miramar has been a hard-working stop on the Northern California rock-club circuit for more than twenty years. Like the jazz spot Bach Dancing and Dynamite Society down the road, the Miramar operates outside the purview of metropolitan San Francisco, so the club frequently plays host to both up-and-comers and over-the-hillers, occasionally landing an out-of-town preview looking to take beyond the glare of big-city publicity. David Crosby, fresh from a Texas prison, played his first show after serving a year on drug charges in 1986 at the remote spot.

Chateau Liberté
22700 Old Santa Cruz Highway, Ben Lomond

A former stagecoach stop turned biker bar, the Chateau was home to the nascent Doobie Brothers, who kept the rent paid during the lean, early days by playing every other weekend, usually alternating with Hot Tuna, at this colorful roadside hostelery. Manager Bruce Cohn remembers taking guns and knives away from the clientele as they passed through the portals, after they paid their $2 admission. The all-wood building on stilts was originally built in 1865 and was a notorious speakeasy during Prohibition, but burned to the ground during the seventies.

171

The Catalyst
1011 Pacific Avenue, Santa Cruz

Neil Young country, this former bowling alley has hosted a wide variety of his various incarnations and flights of fancy, from unannounced performances by Young with Crazy Horse to his short-lived romance with a group called The Ducks, from his ten-man blues band to solo acoustic. In operation since 1976, the Catalyst has been able to consistently attract many headliners looking for a nearby date after playing a metropolitan Bay Area concert, in addition to nurturing the always lively local Santa Cruz music scene.

Monterey County Fairgrounds
2004 Fairgrounds Road, Monterey

Site of the Monterey Jazz Festival every September since 1958, the horse-show arena is mostly remembered for the weekend of June 16–18, 1967, when the Monterey Pop Festival was staged in this bucolic setting. Although the fixed seating in the arena itself held only seventy-five hundred ticket-holders, more than twenty thousand ticketless youth descended on this sleepy seaside city for the event. Celebrated in the film, *Monterey Pop*, and with at least one book and various live recordings culled from engineer Wally Heider's tapes over the years, the pop fest launched the careers of Jimi Hendrix, Janis Joplin (who appeared as a member of Big Brother and the Holding Company), and Otis Redding, among others. Over the years, other events staged at the tree-lined fairgrounds have included the 1964 Monterey Folk Festival, where a young Bob Dylan made his first West Coast appearance, and "Tribal Stomp," a 1975 two-day affair produced by Chet Helms of the Avalon Ballroom, where fewer than five hundred fans showed up for a program that mixed the reggae of Peter Tosh, the punk of The Clash, and sixties rock by Lee Michaels and the Chambers Brothers.

Index

cover photographs: Janis Joplin House (1970, photo by Greg Peterson), Jazz Workshop (1963, photo by Peter Breinig), Jerry Garcia (1983, photo by Steve Ringman). **back cover/author photograph:** Deanne Fitzmaurice.

chapter opener photographs: pp. 16–17, Jazz Workshop (1963, photo by Peter Breinig), The Cellar (1958, photo by Gordon Peters), Bimbo's 365 Club (1960, photo by Ralph D. Demeree), The Condor (1973, photographer unknown); pp. 44–45, Polo Fields (1991, photo by Scott Sommerdorf), Jerry Garcia (1983, photo by Steve Ringman), Grace Slick (1971, photographer unknown); pp. 62–63, Loew's Warfield (photographer unknown), Billie Holliday (1949, photo by Duke Downey), Market Street (1969, photographer unknown); pp. 94–95, Holy City Zoo (1987, photo by Tom Levy), Cow Palace (1941, photographer unknown), St. Francis Fountain (1995, photo by Keta Bill Selvin), Winterland (1972, photo by Dave Randolph); pp. 114–115, Keystone Berkeley (1984, photo by Jerry Telfer), Concord Pavilion (1977, photographer unknown), Paramount Theater (1973, photographer unknown); pp. 142–143, Janis Joplin House (1970, photo by Greg Peterson), Village Music (photo by Mush Emmons/courtesy Village Music); pp. 160–161, Shoreline Amphitheatre (1986, photo by Eric Luse), Circle Star Theater (1986, photo by Bryan Moss).

Index